Sustainable Public Sector Finance in Latin America

A Conference Presented by the
Latin America Research Group

November 1–2, 1999

RESEARCH DEPARTMENT
FEDERAL RESERVE BANK *of* ATLANTA

Additional copies are available through the Atlanta Fed's Web site at
http://www.frbatlanta.org or from the Public Affairs Department,
telephone 404.521.8020

ISBN 0-9624159-2-8

Printed in the United States of America

Contents

FOREWORD
Jack Guynn v

INTRODUCTION
Robert Eisenbeis vii

PATTERNS IN PUBLIC SECTOR ACCOUNTS 1
Elizabeth McQuerry, Michael Chriszt, and Stephen Kay

POLITICAL CONSTRAINTS ON SUSTAINABLE PUBLIC SECTOR
DEVELOPMENT IN LATIN AMERICA 29
Lawrence S. Graham

COMMENTS: Kurt Weyland 48

THE POLITICS OF ADMINISTRATIVE REFORM:
INTRACTABLE DILEMMAS AND IMPROBABLE SOLUTIONS 53
Ben Ross Schneider

COMMENTS: Andrés Fontana 73

CONFRONTING FISCAL IMBALANCES VIA INTERTEMPORAL ECONOMICS,
POLITICS, AND JUSTICE: THE CASE OF COLOMBIA 77
Juan Carlos Echeverry-Garzón and Verónica Navas-Ospina

COMMENTS: Arturo C. Porzecanski 100

PANEL DISCUSSION ON CAPITAL MARKETS AND DEFICIT FINANCE 103
CAPITAL MARKETS AND DEFICIT FINANCE IN BRAZIL 104
Fábio de Oliveira Barbosa
FINANCING DEFICITS IN PERU 116
Carlos Boloña

PANEL DISCUSSION ON INTERNATIONAL LENDING AND CAPITAL FLOWS .. 125
Francisco Gil-Díaz 126
Graham Stock 134

COMMENTS: Robert Eisenbeis 151

SPEECHES 155
PROSPECTS AND DILEMMAS FOR SUSTAINABLE SOCIAL SECTOR
FUNDING IN LATIN AMERICA 156
   Ann Helwege

ADMINISTRATIVE REFORM IN BRAZIL 165
   Cláudia Costin

ABOUT THE AUTHORS 171

Foreword

JACK GUYNN
Federal Reserve Bank of Atlanta

Fiscal policy is at the very core of the profound economic transformation under way in Latin America. While price stabilization and liberalizing reforms have placed regional economies in a much more competitive position over the past two decades, the need for additional reform efforts—so-called second generation reforms like fiscal policy—is increasingly apparent.

Because sound fiscal policy is key to viable monetary policy and sustainable economic growth, few issues are as critical to the region's economic future. This encompassing relevance is the reason the Federal Reserve Bank of Atlanta chose to sponsor a conference on sustainable public sector finance in Latin America, which took place on November 1 and 2, 1999. While our job is the supervision of the U.S. financial sector and the formulation of domestic monetary policy, the reality is that it is no longer possible to think of economic policy—be it monetary policy or supervisory policy—in purely domestic terms. The Federal Reserve's mandate is indeed domestic, but the setting in which we carry out that mandate is increasingly global.

We are well aware that resolving fiscal imbalances can be politically as well as economically difficult. By its very nature, this policy arena involves complex trade-offs, presenting both short-term sacrifices and long-term benefits. Indeed, getting our own fiscal house in order here in the United States was an arduous and lengthy process. But it is now clear that our improving fiscal picture has been an important component in the economic prosperity the United States currently enjoys. Reductions in our government budget deficit have contributed to the stable inflation outlook and have allowed for lower interest rates, which facilitate everything from greater private sector investment to more favorable terms for home mortgages. These in turn boost overall economic activity, which itself contributes to an improving fiscal environment. Although I should not depict it as an economic panacea—which it is not—prudent fiscal policy can provide a virtuous circle of sorts, reinforcing its own benefits for the macro economy.

However, it is also true that the time needed to carry out reforms has become a bit of a luxury item, especially in the context of global financial markets and emerging economies. Financial market forces can reward countries pursuing sound policies, but those same forces are also increasingly quick to punish economies with sustained economic imbalances—particularly in the fiscal arena.

I would like to acknowledge all the conference participants for their superior contributions and enthusiastic discussion during the meeting. I would also like to thank the staff in the Bank's Research Department for their efforts in putting together this excellent program.

Finally, our sincere hope, in making this volume available, is that it will be useful for students and policymakers as both a resource and a record of innovative approaches to understanding fiscal policy.

Introduction

ROBERT EISENBEIS
Federal Reserve Bank of Atlanta

In order to address the broad policy implications and wide-ranging nature of fiscal policy, participants in the conference on Sustainable Public Sector Finance in Latin America were asked to explore the issue from various angles, employing different disciplinary approaches. The following overview of the papers and presentations from the conference provides insight into some of these perspectives.

The basic policy elements of sustainable public sector finance are presented in the introductory paper by Elizabeth McQuerry, Michael Chriszt, and Stephen Kay. Economic fundamentals and the notion of policy credibility are explored through a review of existing research on fiscal policy in Latin America. The authors also examine how Latin American governments have performed in achieving their fiscal policy objectives and provide a selected research bibliography that will be a useful guide for scholars.

Larry Graham offers a comprehensive, historical survey of four key countries. In analyzing the developmental paths of Argentina, Brazil, Mexico, and Venezuela, Dr. Graham outlines four distinct political trends, which to varying degrees have been manifested throughout the region and which continue to shape contemporary policy outcomes in the region.

Ben Ross Schneider explores why administrative reform has been so problematic in the region. His analysis draws insight from institutional economics to examine the specific political dynamics of the life cycle of reform, from elections to final implementation. The analysis has important policy implications for administrative reform efforts as well as for other types of economic and political reforms.

Juan Carlos Echeverry and Verónica Navas evaluate fiscal policy in Colombia, analyzing public sector net worth using both flow and stock approaches. The authors argue that the feasibility of a particular fiscal package depends not only on a sound economic approach but also on the establishment of a new political and judicial approach to the decision-making process that would avoid the type of institutional conflicts that have occurred in some countries. Echeverry and Navas also argue that policy should be directed toward the pursuit of a dynamic equilibrium related to public sector net worth as opposed to explicit debt and deficit targets.

Deficit finance is the subject of a panel featuring remarks by two distinguished practitioners of debt management in Latin America. Carlos Boloña, who served as Minister of Economy and Finance in Peru from 1991 to 1993, shares insight from his experiences as finance minister during a very difficult period in the country's economic and political history. His tenure was also the period during which Peru effectively came to terms with many debt-management issues. The discussion by Fábio de Oliveira Barbosa, the Secretary of the Treasury in Brazil, maps out the Brazilian government's debt strategy. His presentation provides important insight for countries seeking to establish and maintain access to international credit lines as they build domestic credit markets. The Brazilian experience also illustrates how fiscal policy and global economic conditions can work at cross-purposes, presenting policymakers with even larger budgetary challenges.

The panel on international lending and capital flows features the views of two prominent investment practitioners. The assertion by Francisco Gil-Díaz that all foreign debt in emerging market economies—whether held by the sovereign and in private hands—is a sovereign liability is a sobering reminder that the rapid increase in capital flows and international markets has wide-ranging implications. At the same time, Graham Stock notes in his paper that creditor analysis of emerging market lending is essentially the same as other credit analysis: countries that meet these criteria will find ready access to international capital markets while those that fail to meet them must resort to much more onerous terms.

Conference participants were also fortunate to hear the views of two distinguished speakers. Ann Helwege shared her research with Eliana Cardoso on how Latin American governments have fared with poverty alleviation efforts and outlined the prospects for future efforts in an environment of resource constraints. Cláudia Costin provided the keynote address from her first-hand experience with state reform as Brazil's secretary of state for administration and government property. The Brazilian example illustrates many of the multifaceted challenges facing reformers.

The conference also benefited from a very learned and enthusiastic group of participants—encompassing viewpoints from academia, banking, government, and the private sector—who shared their perspectives and experiences on fiscal policy. This depth allowed participants to discuss public sector finance along a broad spectrum during the two-day conference.

At the end of the proceedings, participants were asked to identify the primary areas on which further research on fiscal policy would most fruitfully be focused. Three areas figured prominently in this discussion: (1) the need for greater understanding of the role of institutions in fiscal policy reform, especially as regards constitutional reform, congress, and transparency of the policy process; (2) several issues, such as tax reform, income distribution, foreign direct investment, hidden public debt, and pension liabilities, were seen as needing further study and specification to determine the significance of their role in fiscal policy reform. Finally, the need for a greater understanding of the relationship between fiscal policy and dollarization was cited.

Patterns in Latin American
Public Sector Accounts

Patterns in Latin American Public Sector Accounts

ELIZABETH MCQUERRY, MICHAEL CHRISZT, AND STEPHEN KAY
Federal Reserve Bank of Atlanta[1]

The existence of large public sector deficits in some Latin American countries has received considerable attention over the past few years. Indeed, the recent trend in public sector accounts in many countries has been toward larger deficits rather than a general movement toward shrinking shortfalls, despite the gains achieved in many countries during the early part of the nineties. Moreover, weaknesses in government accounts and the failure to further extend liberalizing reforms to the state apparatus itself have made Latin American countries especially vulnerable to financial market swings. In the environment of the Asian economic crisis and growing investor uncertainty toward emerging markets, these swings have helped to increase deficits and government indebtedness and, in some cases, have helped to precipitate currency crises.

From the perspective of the United States, this topic has considerable relevance. The growing relationship between Latin America and the United States means that, more than ever, events in Latin America have important economic and financial implications for the U.S. economy. Public sector finance can significantly influence macroeconomic performance and play a role in triggering financial difficulties. It is therefore critical for U.S. business and policymakers to know what the issues and problems are and what solutions are available.

This article provides an overview of the subject, reviews trends in fiscal policy throughout the region, and offers a concise, analytical review of how Latin American governments have performed in this area. The overview examines salient areas of concern, individual country experiences, and some of the key challenges facing governments in the region. Data in this paper are largely limited to Argentina, Brazil, Chile, Colombia, Ecuador, Mexico, Peru, and Venezuela.

Before entering a discussion of the literature on fiscal policy, it is important to note that comparisons across countries present difficult problems. There are wide variations in methodology and definition. Although country data managers and multilateral financial institutions are working to improve data quality and standardization, these limitations should be considered in multicountry analyses. Another issue is missing data; the absence of years in time series data makes longer-term comparisons difficult. The lack of data on smaller countries may obscure important complexities.

Literature on Fiscal Policy in Latin America

While research on Latin America is a relatively recent addition to fiscal policy literature, it falls squarely within scholars' established efforts to identify constraints on regional development and improve economic outcomes. Much research has sought to analyze structural shortcomings in the region's particular economic framework. The well-known work by Cardoso and Faletto (1979) on dependent development is but one example. Although impediments to development have often been identified as exogenous in the past, these works also sought to diagnose why Latin American economies often failed to operate efficiently and fulfill basic societal needs.

As regional governments began to open their economies, scholars began to identify endogenous impediments to development. The bureaucratic apparatus of the state in Latin America was identified as a primary factor inhibiting efficient outcomes in both the public and private sectors. Bresser Pereira (1996) looks at Latin America's economic crisis as a crisis of the state, linking reform of the state to the success of economic reform. In recent years, research has focused on government fiscal outcomes due to the persistence of unbalanced public sector accounts. Price stabilization in Latin America allowed scholars to approach the study of fiscal policy with new rigor. The taming of inflation, which served to diminish the impact of poor fiscal outcomes, also allowed public sector accounts to be evaluated on a planning basis for the first time in many years.

In contrast, examination of fiscal questions in the developed countries has been the subject of extensive investigation. Spiraling expenditure and burgeoning deficits in the Organization for Economic Cooperation and Development (OECD) countries during the late seventies and early eighties stimulated a rich body of work exploring the impact of deficits on public sector debt, interest rates, exchange regimes, and macroeconomic

performance. While this body of work most accurately describes the processes and dynamics of public sector adjustment in developed economies,
many macroeconomic and political considerations are generally applica-
ble to open economies.

There are, nevertheless, important limitations in applying the models and
theoretical approaches elaborated in the context of developed countries.
Chief among these are the challenges presented by the historical and institutional development of the various nation states and the differing structure of
economies in Latin America. While OECD countries are much more industrialized and have a broader and more reliable revenue base, Latin American
countries rely more heavily on volatile export commodity production and are
more likely to access international capital markets at less favorable terms.
Some of these limitations were noted three decades ago when Hart (1970)
argued that the predominant economic models were neither sophisticated
nor dynamic enough to capture the reality of the region's fiscal systems.

Two works that examine fiscal issues on a regional basis are particularly salient. Perry and Herrera (1994) offer a pioneering effort to evaluate
issues affecting public sector adjustment throughout Latin America. This
study examines the impact of decentralization, privatization, and tax
reform on fiscal policy; it notes, as would later work, that government fiscal policy often produces suboptimal outcomes because general economy
and public sector accounts tend to work at cross-purposes.

Institutional issues have also entered the focus. The 1997 annual report
from the Inter-American Development Bank (IDB) contains an excellent
discussion of the dominant trends and varied constraints on fiscal policy.
One of the chief findings in the report is a tendency toward procyclical fiscal outcomes in Latin America, where government spending practices
tend to amplify (rather than mitigate or offset) the natural tendencies of
recessions and periods of growth. In practice, this procyclical pattern
means that governments tend to cut spending during recessions, thereby
deepening the recession, rather than supporting the economy via
increased government spending. The report also notes a tendency for public sector accounts to deteriorate during electoral periods as incumbent
governments attempt to influence electoral outcomes. These findings
highlight the institutional constraints on balanced budgeting faced by
Latin American nations, focusing in particular on the nature of the state,
the problems of policy decisions for countries undergoing democratic
transitions, and the dilemmas in federalist political systems.[2]

Another perspective looks at public sector adjustment as a "fiscal
covenant" and seeks to broaden the scope beyond economic cycles and

institutions. Describing the "basic socio-political agreement that legit-imizes the role of the State and establishes the areas and scope of govern-ment responsibility in the economic and social spheres," the fiscal covenant involves "consolidating the ongoing fiscal adjustment process, raising the productivity of public management, making fiscal activity more transparent, promoting social equity and encouraging the development of democratic institutions" (CEPAL 1998, 1). The fiscal covenant illustrates a new approach to improving public sector adjustment, emphasizing a broad-based endeavor to improve public sector output and the overall quality of government.

The research comprised in this literature is too vast to discuss in this brief survey. Many works focus on the particular problems preventing Latin American countries from achieving greater fiscal equilibrium and have thus inspired work on obstacles specific to the region. Some are country studies while others explore the particular set of problems faced by each economy given its historical and institutional makeup. Others look at broader issues affecting many countries in the region. The select-ed research bibliography lists many works in this growing literature. The notion of sustainability, an all-important concern in public sector finance, is also addressed in this literature and in the next section.

The Elements of Sustainable Public Sector Finance

An important trend in most Latin American countries over the past decade has been a tendency toward an improved budget balance as measured by the primary balance (revenues minus expenditures only). Indeed, the pri-mary deficit in Latin American and Caribbean countries was substantially reduced to an unweighted average of 1.7 percent of gross domestic product (GDP) in 1997 from 5.7 percent in 1988. Chart 1 demonstrates these trends.

The major economies in Latin America performed slightly better than did the region as a whole. Whereas the unweighted average for all twenty-six countries improved 4 percentage points over the decade, the unweighted average for these eight countries improved 4.3 percentage points, falling from a deficit of almost 5 percent of GDP in 1988 to an aver-age primary deficit of less than one percent (0.6) of GDP in 1997. Also, the bulk of the improvement occurred in the early part of the decade, followed by some deterioration in the latter half.[3]

These results place the region in a position only modestly worse than the advanced industrial countries. According to the International

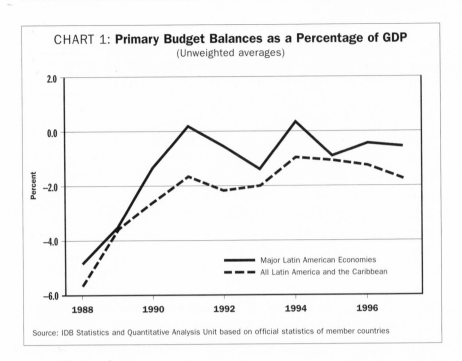

CHART 1: **Primary Budget Balances as a Percentage of GDP**
(Unweighted averages)

Source: IDB Statistics and Quantitative Analysis Unit based on official statistics of member countries

Monetary Fund (IMF), the average general government balance for the advanced economies was a deficit of 1.0 percent of GDP in 1997 (International Monetary Fund 1999). By comparison, the larger economies in Latin America fared even better, as their average deficit was only 0.6 percent of GDP. Why then does the fiscal position of Latin American governments receive so much scrutiny?

The answer lies mainly in the region's much greater potential to undergo rapid economic swings, making it susceptible to major shifts in budgetary outcomes. These swings, which often necessitate additional debt financing, are reflected in the real economy as well as in government accounts. The macroeconomic environment in Latin America is "about two to three times as volatile as the industrial economies, and more volatile than any region other than Africa and the Middle East" (Gavin and others 1996, 1).

Gavin and others also argue that using the primary balance (as a percentage of GDP) as a measure may underestimate the size of the fiscal deficit in Latin America. Table 1 demonstrates how deficits would be substantially higher if other indicators were utilized. One of these indicators measures financial depth in the national economy through the share of M2 (a broad measure of the money supply) in GDP, allowing an examination of "the average fiscal deficit relative to the domestic financial system that will be called upon to finance" the budget shortfall (Gavin and others 1996, 4). This exercise found that deficits in Latin America were almost three times larger than the average for OECD countries over a twenty-five year period (1970–94).

A second indicator that may more accurately capture the dimensions of fiscal deficits in Latin America is the size of the deficit "in comparison to the ability to effect a fiscal adjustment" (Gavin and others 1996, 4). This measure compares the deficit with total tax revenue. Here, while the differences between Latin American and OECD countries were not as large as those indicated by the financial depth measure (M2), the implications for Latin America are much more onerous. Over the period from 1970 to 1994, the primary deficit-to-tax revenue ratio was 21 percent in Latin America as compared with a deficit of only 15 percent in OECD countries (Gavin and others 1996, 3–4).[4]

A variety of reasons underlie the return to primary deficits. Low economic growth, recessions, and the failure to make sufficient spending cuts would top a list of factors contributing to the growth of budget deficits. Nevertheless, a larger question remains: Why, despite so many efforts over the past two decades, have regional governments not been able to implement effective and sustainable fiscal adjustment? Ter-Minassian and Schwartz note that adjustment efforts in the 1980s shared a handful of factors that tended to limit their success. They concluded

TABLE 1: **Consolidated Central Government Fiscal Surplus, Latin America and OECD Countries**

	1970–94		1990–94	
	OECD	L.A.	OECD	L.A.
Overall Surplus				
Relative to GDP	−3.8	−3.9	−3.8	−1.6
Relative to financial depth	−5.1	−14.9	−4.1	−4.5
Relative to fiscal revenue	−15.0	−21.0	−13.5	−8.0
Primary Surplus				
Relative to GDP	−1.1	0.6	0.0	7.5
Relative to financial depth	−1.5	2.2	0.0	20.6
Relative to fiscal revenue	−4.5	3.1	0.0	36.6

All figures refer to population-weighted averages of underlying country data. In some countries data are missing for some years, in which case we used all available observations in the relevant time period.

Source: Gavin and others 1996, 3.

that "their foremost common characteristic is perhaps the fact that they all failed to signal convincingly a fundamental change of the economic policy regime and therefore lacked credibility" (1997, 10). The authors attribute this lack of credibility to "inconsistent policy mixes," "excessive reliance on endogenous factors," "failure to implement fundamental fiscal reforms," and the "lack of needed complementary structural reforms" (1997, 10–11). Despite some improvements, many of these factors still characterize fiscal policy in the region and, to the extent that they exist, continue to mitigate against credibility and sustainable adjustment.

Tanzi (1990) asserts that fiscal adjustment is but one component of a larger process of economic stabilization being carried out by most countries. Fiscal stabilization involves "(i) measuring the extent of the existing fiscal disequilibria; (ii) determining the size of the fiscal adjustment needed; (iii) selecting appropriate high-quality fiscal adjustment measures; and, finally, (iv) sequencing correctly the implementation of the selected measures" (cited in Ter-Minassian 1997, 5). Achievement of these policies must take place within a comprehensive strategy of structural economic adjustment. In this sense, credibility is more likely to be determined by a larger set of policies and economic goals than fiscal policy alone. However, now that many governments have already put other structural adjustment measures into place, fiscal policy has become the cornerstone of economic policy credibility.

Thus, the notion of sustainable public sector finance connotes more than producing short-term surpluses through auspicious macroeconomic fundamentals or harsh cuts. It also implies identifying the debt burden that is manageable for each individual country's output and spending needs— an achievement that necessarily stipulates a medium-term horizon. International comparisons suggest that viable debt ratios may vary by region and by country. While Latin American countries are generally considered to be highly indebted, most of them would satisfy the debt criteria established in the Maastricht Treaty.[5] Among the eight major economies considered here, only Ecuador had a ratio of external debt to gross domestic product (GDP) exceeding 60 percent. The average external debt ratio in all Latin American countries was considerably lower, at 33.6 percent according to 1997 data.[6]

The recent pattern in debt held by the public sector in Latin America can be seen in Chart 2, which measures external debt relative to gross national product (GNP). The trend reveals that total external debt rose steadily in the 1980s and then began to decline in the late 1980s and into the early 1990s, leveling off by mid-decade. Worsening of the debt levels in the 1980s resulted from (1) the rise in international interest rates beginning in 1981, (2) deterioration in the terms of trade for many countries and resulting devaluations, and (3) serious financial crises that resulted in significant government-sponsored bank bailouts. The improvement in the 1990s can be traced to efforts to reduce government spending in many countries, the Brady Plan and Paris Club deals that reduced external debt, a return to positive economic growth, and a reduction in interest rates. As a result, the overall debt-to-GNP levels for the major Latin American countries declined from 65 percent of GNP in 1987 to just below 37 percent by 1998.

Nevertheless, despite these comparatively lower levels, the interest and principal payments on the debt weigh heavily on government accounts throughout the region. In 1997, the average debt service ratio was 33.8 percent, meaning that interest payments on foreign debt were equivalent to one-third of the country's exports of goods and services. Argentina (58.7 percent), Brazil (57.4 percent), and Mexico (32.4 percent) carried the highest burdens (World Bank 1999).

A widely shared notion of improving public sector financing calls for placing the ratio of external debt to the size of the economy on a downward trajectory. How much adjustment is enough, and how is successful adjustment measured? The definition by Alesina and Perotti (1995) provides a baseline. A successful adjustment can be measured by a reduction

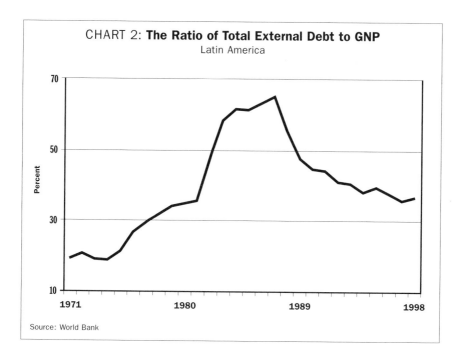

CHART 2: **The Ratio of Total External Debt to GNP**
Latin America

Source: World Bank

of at least five percentage points within the three years after implementing the adjustment. As Chart 1 shows, most governments in Latin America have achieved substantial reductions in their external debt burden. However, much of this improvement was due to the previously mentioned debt-restructuring efforts. In the absence of these interventions, most governments would have had some difficulty keeping the external debt ratio on a downward trajectory or keeping the ratio at a stable level for prolonged periods.

In the uncertain environment in which many Latin American governments operate, policymakers must often resort to new deficit financing and pay the higher premiums demanded by market participants in exchange for the increase in sovereign risk (from rising debt levels) or transfer risk (from the possibility of depreciation in the foreign exchange rate). Indeed, "policymakers in Latin America have typically faced a loss of confidence and thus intensified borrowing constraints during bad macroeconomic times. The loss of market access makes it impossible to run a countercyclical fiscal policy, at least in bad times. A full description of Latin American fiscal outcomes needs to account for this *precarious creditworthiness*" (emphasis in original) (Gavin and Perotti 1997, 40).

Recent work calls attention to the danger presented by short-term external debt. Table 2 shows a ratio of short-term foreign debt to international reserves as a measure of liquidity for the major Latin economies (Russia and South Korea are included for comparison). This measure is similar to that developed by Chang and Velasco (1998) but also includes

TABLE 2: **Latin American International Liquidity**

	1997	1998	June 1999
Argentina	1.88	1.63	1.70
Brazil	1.12	1.16	1.20
Chile	0.66	0.60	0.64
Colombia	0.81	0.96	1.00
Ecuador	1.13	1.50	1.54
Mexico	1.18	1.06	1.05
Peru	0.64	0.80	0.83
Venezuela	0.40	0.48	0.50
Russia	2.55	2.31	2.25
South Korea	3.25	0.82	0.69

Source: BIS, IMF, OECD, and the Federal Reserve Bank of Atlanta (based on measures developed by Chang and Velasco 1998)

debt securities issued abroad and nonbank trade credits in the short-term debt indicator. A ratio of one means that there would be exactly enough in reserves to pay off a country's foreign creditors if they decided not to roll over the debt. A ratio higher than one indicates a shortfall.

The table shows that five of the eight major Latin American economies had ratios of either one or more at mid-1999. In addition, it shows that the ratios in most countries are climbing—in the case of Ecuador, rather rapidly. Chang and Velasco's research shows that this ratio is a good indicator of possible international liquidity problems; countries with a high ratio of short-term debt to international reserves can face problems if investors begin to shy away from their debt, which is what happened in Asia in 1997 and Russia in 1998.

Another consideration in the debt question is the recent increase in domestic debt held by the public sector. Macroeconomic stabilization in the 1990s has led to increased domestic financing throughout Latin America. Although external borrowing provides the bulk of financing needs in most countries in the region, domestic debt has been increasing. In 1998, public sector domestic debt in Argentina, Colombia, Ecuador, Peru, and Venezuela was modest, equaling no more than 15 percent of GDP. In Colombia and Ecuador, however, domestic issuance had doubled since 1995. In spite of these increases, the limited nature of capital markets and banking systems, as well as low domestic savings, means that domestic borrowing is not a significant option in most Latin countries. Brazil, Chile, and Mexico do rely on domestic financing. The total amount of domestic debt issued by the public sector in these three countries represented 54, 39, and 27 percent, respectively (Chase Securities 1999).

While the default risk on sovereign domestic debt is generally quite low, and transfer risk is not present, the rapid increase in public sector domestic debt presents potential concerns. For countries that do issue domestic debt, the danger of short-term issuance is also present. Recall that in the case of Mexico in 1994, it was the refusal of domestic debt holders to roll over their paper that contributed to the peso crisis.

Some studies suggest that focusing on the debt burden provides an incomplete indicator of sustainable public sector finance. One analysis asserts that the debt-to-GDP ratio is an incomplete indicator of fiscal sustainability because it measures government solvency more than the sustainability of the government's fiscal policy. Horne states that "public debt ratios and sustainability indicators are not conceptually equivalent (the former measures the actual or ex post ratio of the outstanding stock of public indebtedness while the latter are ex ante measures of the required permanent fiscal adjustment needed to stabilize the base year public debt ratio)" (1991, 18).

Solvency is also critiqued by Borchardt, Rial, and Sarmiento, who argue that, by itself, solvency does not address the range of relevant indicators. Sustainability is a much broader concept that locates public sector accounts firmly within the real economy. A sustainable policy is one in which "government spending programs are consistent with the possibility of obtaining revenue through taxes and/or debt financing, without endangering political economy goals, or the fulfillment of present and future obligations" (1998, 22). Employing Blanchard's (1990) methodology, Borchardt, Rial, and Sarmiento assert that "fiscal policy is sustainable if the real debt does not grow more rapidly than the difference between the real interest rate and the growth rate of the economy" (1998, 22).

This review of major trends in public sector finances strongly suggests that a downward trend in the ratio of external debt is not likely to be sufficient if policy sustainability is the goal. The comparatively low debt ratios in most Latin American countries demonstrate that their manageable or sustainable debt ratio may be considerably lower than that in the industrial countries. Similarly, Latin America's experience calls into question the notion that successful fiscal consolidation can be determined by a sustained downward trend in the external debt ratio in more volatile economies.

The increasing interdependence of economies also poses challenges to countries with fiscal problems. Markets can effectively transfer risk, or perceived risk, across national boundaries in a matter of minutes. Furthermore, national finances may be subject to detrimental market oscillations from other countries with unsustainable polices. This dynamic implies the need for a credible economic policy mix that will balance public sector accounts in the medium term as well as help to shield the domestic economy from short-term market contagion. If any of these conditions are lacking, adjustment is likely to be ephemeral or to fail completely. Short-term solutions are not likely to be sustainable, and they carry heavy social costs that can only exacerbate the social deficit. In other words, sustainable public sector finance demands both sound fundamentals and policy credibility in order to create the necessary circumstances for a successful and sustainable adjustment.

The next section sets forth some of the reasons that sustainable public sector finance is a shared goal among countries. After all, deficits are not necessarily bad. Capital expenditure and other productive spending are more commonly thought of as investments than deficits. However, when spending on the basic operations of government outpaces revenue for extended periods of time, or if deficits in some areas continuously pilfer money from other areas, budget deficits serve as a structural constraint on economies, siphoning away current and future revenue that could otherwise be used for developmental purposes. Also, government budget deficits are increasingly viewed as a liability that affects the creditworthiness of not only the sovereign but also all economic entities operating within its territory.

Why Budget Deficits Matter

This section briefly reviews some basic economic principles with regard to the effects of budget deficits on an economy. The most important factor to consider is that budget deficits reduce national saving, that is, the sum of public saving and private saving (after-tax income that is saved rather than spent). Both public and private savings result from monies remaining after necessary expenses have been met. If the government spends more than it takes in, it cannot generate savings and must sometimes resort to increasing taxes. Therefore a government that has a budget deficit reduces the total national saving.

Some economists have argued that when a government runs a deficit, private savers will boost their savings to compensate for the decrease in public saving, thereby offsetting the negative effect of the budget deficit on national saving. However, the preponderance of evidence shows that an increase in private savings does not wholly compensate for the decrease in public savings. The effect of a budget deficit on national saving is not a zero-sum game just because a decline in public saving is at least partially offset by an increase in private saving. A tax cut, for example, reduces public saving. Households would see their income rise, and they would likely spend part of this increase and save part. The portion spent would generate some tax revenue for the government, thereby increasing public saving, and the portion not spent would increase private saving. The bottom line is that a budget deficit leads to a decline in national saving, but not at a one-to-one ratio.

A decline in national saving has a negative impact on the overall economy. Ball and Mankiw's (1995) description of some basic accounting illustrates this point:

$$S = Y - C - G,$$

where S = national saving, Y = gross domestic product, C = consumption, and G = government purchases. The next equation to consider is the one that divides GDP into four spending categories:

$$Y = C + I + G + NX,$$

where Y = GDP, C = consumption, I = investment, G = government purchases, and NX = net exports. Substituting the second expression for Y in the first equation yields

$$S = I + NX.$$

If a budget deficit leads to a decline in national saving, and if national saving is equal to investment plus net exports, the effect of a decline in national saving must be a decline in investment or net exports, or a combination of both.

How exactly does a budget deficit and resulting decline in national saving translate into a decline in investment or net exports? A decline in investment can be described as resulting from increased interest rates. Interest rates rise because a decline in national savings results in a decrease in the supply of loans to private borrowers; as savings decline, there is simply less money available to make loans. The decline in the supply of loans increases the cost, which pushes up the interest rate. Faced with higher interest rates, private borrowers who wish to borrow funds to invest may curtail their investment plans.

Budget deficits and a decline in national saving affect net exports through the interest rate channel as well. Higher interest rates attract more investors, both domestic and foreign. Since investors who wish to purchase assets of another country must first purchase that country's currency in order to make the transaction, demand for the currency increases. Increased demand results in a higher price for the currency—in other words, the currency appreciates. The stronger currency means that domestic goods are more expensive for foreigners and foreign goods are cheaper for domestic consumers. The resulting increase in imports and decline in exports worsens or turns the trade account toward deficit.

If protracted, declines in investment and net exports have a negative impact on national output. On the investment side, persistent declines reduce growth in a country's capital stock, which in turn reduces a country's ability to produce goods and services. Persistent net export deficits also hurt output as more and more income from domestic production flows overseas to finance the deficit. So, persistent budget deficits lead to a reduction in output because less is produced, because less of the production stays at home, or because of a combination of both.

The Key Variables

This section takes the analysis one step further by looking at some of the leading influences on government accounts. The discussion examines revenue and expenditure as factors that determine government budget balance in the short term as well as affect the long-term sustainability of public sector finance. As a foundation for considering these two variables, we first examine the importance of the institutional context in determining fiscal outcomes.

Institutions. Research on the relationship between institutions and fiscal deficits suggests that fiscal policy outcomes result in part from institutional design. Policy making is, of course, a complex process that is contingent upon numerous political and economic variables, and there is no agreed-upon set of optimal institutions. Stein, Talvi, and Grisanti (1998) divide budgetary institutions into three categories based upon numerical constraints, procedural rules, and transparency. Balanced-budget laws, fiscal targets, and debt ceilings constitute numerical constraints. Procedural rules refer to whether or not budgets are set in hierarchical or procedural arrangements. Hierarchical rules give greater power to the executive branch while collegial rules provide a greater balance between the executive branch and the legislature. Finally, they examine the transparency of the budget process, that is, the extent to which the budget contains an accurate projection of revenue, debt, and expenditures. In their index of budgetary institutions (based on an index later published as Alesina and others 1999), the authors conclude that more transparent and hierarchical budget institutions tend to have lower deficit and debt levels. Furthermore, Alesina and others (1999) also conclude that predefined fiscal targets and preapproved debt ceilings may be a good substitute for balanced-budget laws. These findings present evidence of how institutional reform can lead to improved fiscal performance.

Another perspective, found in Stein, Talvi, and Grisanti (1998), examines the relationship between electoral systems and fiscal outcomes. Governments tend to use plurality (also known as first-past-the-post or winner-take-all) systems, in which all the seats go to the winner, or proportional representation systems, in which seats are allocated in proportion to votes received, or a mixture of the two. Within an electoral district, one or more representatives might be elected. (This variable is referred to as district magnitude.) Plurality systems or systems with low district magnitude (such as the United States or United Kingdom, where one representative is elected per district), tend toward two-party systems that elect governments having a majority party in Congress. Proportional representation tends to lead to multiparty coalition governments. The authors conclude that electoral systems characterized by large degrees of proportionality, large district magnitude, and a large degree of political fragmentation tend to have larger governments, larger deficits, and a more procyclical response to the business cycle.

These works suggest that governments pursuing fiscal reform must appraise the role of institutions and consider the extent to which institutional reform might complement fiscal policy reform. The following sections examine fiscal outcomes by breaking them into revenue and expenditure categories and discuss some considerations for the region.

Revenue. The predominant experience among Latin American governments on the revenue side of the budgetary equation is a pattern of erratic increases that often grow more slowly than expenditure and are less sustained by tax collection than in the industrialized countries. Gavin and others (1996) find that the swings in real fiscal revenue are three times greater in Latin America than in the industrialized countries.

Even so, revenue has grown in absolute terms substantially in many countries. Except for Venezuela, where total revenue was actually lower in dollar terms in 1998 than in 1980, the amount collected in the major Latin American economies grew between one and fourfold over the period. As Chart 3 demonstrates, revenue grew fairly steadily, though not without

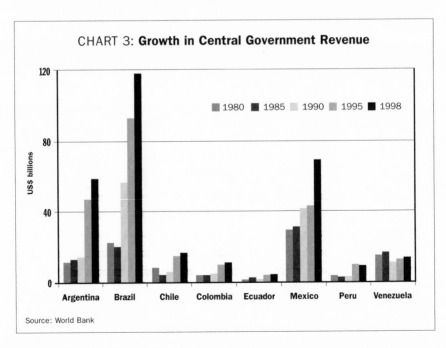

CHART 3: **Growth in Central Government Revenue**

Source: World Bank

some fluctuations, especially in the mid- and late eighties when revenue fell in most countries, only to rebound later.

Relative to the overall size of the economy, however, there has been considerable volatility and variation among countries. These trends can be seen in Charts 4–5. The region's well-known fluctuations in economic

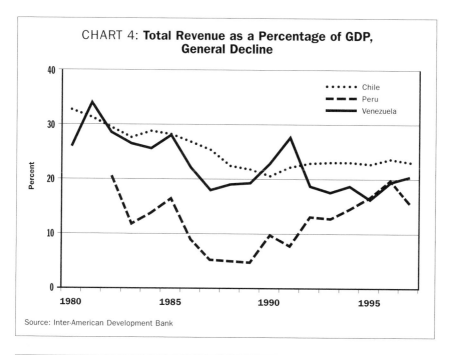

CHART 4: **Total Revenue as a Percentage of GDP, General Decline**

Source: Inter-American Development Bank

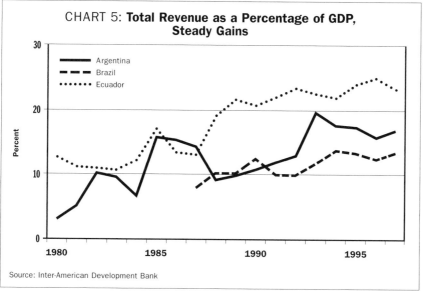

CHART 5: **Total Revenue as a Percentage of GDP, Steady Gains**

Source: Inter-American Development Bank

performance have produced a situation in which growth was punctuated with significant swings, even in the countries for which revenue increased as a percentage of GDP. Argentina, Brazil, and Ecuador were the only countries to experience fairly steady and substantial gains in the ratio of revenue to GDP, the percentage of which grew between twofold and fivefold over the period. In Chile, Peru, and Venezuela, on the other hand, revenue represented a smaller percentage of GDP in 1997 than it had at the onset of the eighties. The revenue-to-GDP ratio remained relatively static in Colombia and Mexico, with both countries maintaining their levels around 12 and 15 percent, respectively, over the time period.

Comparing the region with OECD countries provides a different benchmark for evaluating the revenue side. Gavin and others (1996) make these comparisons using some structural characteristics of consolidated central government revenue in thirteen Latin American countries and twenty-one OECD member countries over a twenty-five year span (1970–94). OECD countries take in more revenue (relative to the size of their economies) and are better at collecting taxes than their counterparts in Latin America. While the more industrialized countries averaged tax revenue collection equivalent to 23.2 percent of GDP, governments in Latin America collected less than two-thirds of that amount (14.7 percent of GDP). The difference is even greater if Brazil and the United States are factored out (1996, 5).

The disparities were especially marked for income tax and social security tax collection; OECD governments collected at least twice the amount taken in by Latin American governments as a percentage of GDP. However, Latin American governments were stronger in some areas, collecting slightly more indirect taxes than in OECD countries. In terms of nontax revenue, Latin governments collected considerably more than their OECD counterparts, averaging 3.2 percent of GDP compared with 2.0 percent in OECD countries.

This study also separated out data for 1990–94, allowing a test for any differences in the structure of revenue after liberalizing reforms had begun to be put into place. Few significant enhancements were apparent. While the ratio of total revenue to GDP increased almost 2 percentage points on average in Latin America, both nontax and tax revenue fell as a percentage of total revenue. Tax revenue dropped to 71.8 percent of total revenue in the 1990–94 period from 79.1 percent during the entire 1970–94 span while nontax revenue fell to 15.9 percent from 17.1 percent of total revenue. Although the scale is much smaller, tax revenue also declined in the OECD countries over the period from 1970 to 1994, dropping from 91.4 percent of total revenue to 90.2 percent from 1990 to 1994 (see Gavin and others 1996, 5).

Expenditure. Expenditure patterns in the region generally reflect a high degree of volatility, although this pattern has been muted somewhat since some countries have achieved price stability. Once high or hyperinflation was halted, governments lost the use of an important adjustment tool. Consequently we see the end of volatility in some countries, with expenditures reaching a plateau in Argentina, Brazil, and Peru over the last several years. This section highlights some of the principle characteristics of expenditure among Latin American countries and then focuses on patterns in social expenditure.

The degree of volatility in nominal government expenditures (as a percentage of GDP) in most countries is striking. The three distinct patterns in our sample can be seen in Charts 6–8. In Argentina, Brazil, and Peru, public expenditures as a percentage of GDP were extremely volatile between 1986 and 1993 but then reached a plateau between 1993 and 1997. In Colombia, Ecuador, and Venezuela, volatility was also present before expenditures began rising throughout the mid-1990s. Chile and Mexico provide a striking contrast, as public expenditures as a percentage of GDP have been in decline. In Chile, after expenditures peaked at 34.1 percent of GDP in 1982, they dropped to a low of 20.3 percent in 1990 and grew very slightly over the

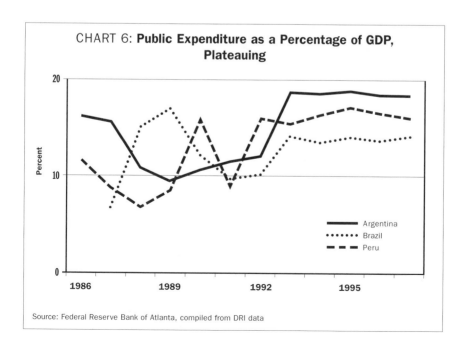

CHART 6: **Public Expenditure as a Percentage of GDP, Plateauing**

Source: Federal Reserve Bank of Atlanta, compiled from DRI data

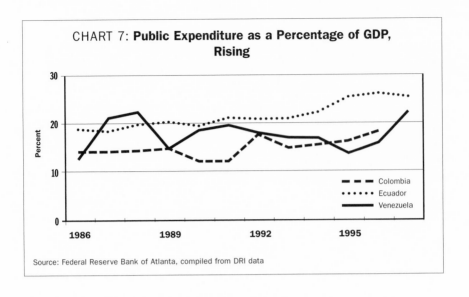

CHART 7: **Public Expenditure as a Percentage of GDP, Rising**

Source: Federal Reserve Bank of Atlanta, compiled from DRI data

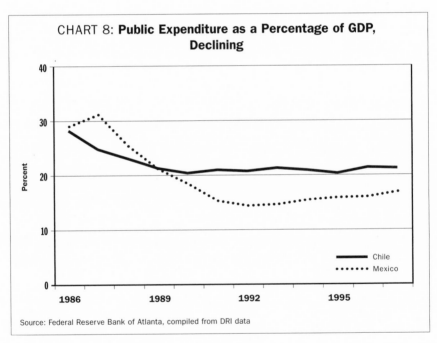

CHART 8: **Public Expenditure as a Percentage of GDP, Declining**

Source: Federal Reserve Bank of Atlanta, compiled from DRI data

1990s. In Mexico, spending peaked at 31.2 percent in 1987 and fell to 14.5 percent in 1992 before rising to 17 percent in 1997.

In Argentina, Brazil, and Peru, the pattern of volatility ended once relative price stability was introduced and expenditures reached a plateau. The plateau effect may reflect the absence of inflation as a means of fiscal adjustment after achieving relative price stability. Previously, inflation often served essentially as a tax or a politically convenient tool, which could be used without regard to legislative approval and allowed governments to reduce the outstanding value of debts and expenditures. After price stabilization, governments faced the more politically problematic task of implementing cuts in public spending. The topping out of public expenditures at peak levels in Argentina and Brazil reflects the degree of difficulty that governments have encountered in making these cuts. In Colombia, Ecuador, and Venezuela, expenditures continued to rise through 1997 and offer no clear evidence that they have topped out. Of this group, oil-dependent Venezuela is the most erratic, showing a sharp rise in expenditures since 1995. These patterns reflect the clear divergence that has taken place in the region with respect to those countries that have cut public expenditures and those that have not. The box describes the region's experience with social security spending, an area of particular concern for policymakers today.

As Gavin and others (1996) note, there are several important differences between spending patterns in Latin America and the OECD countries. In Latin America, interest payments, capital expenditures, and wage payments take on a proportionally greater weight than in the OECD countries. Interest payments are the result of previous borrowing decisions and will rise as interest rates rise. Meanwhile it is politically difficult to reduce wage expenditures. The lower level of social welfare spending in Latin America reflects less-developed social welfare systems, though a wide range of spending levels exists in the region, as discussed below. Also, while Latin American countries tend to have lower transfer payments (that is, transfers and subsidies to state and local governments, decentralized agencies, and state-owned firms) than OECD countries, there is a great deal of divergence among country experiences. Transfer payments have risen dramatically in Mexico while they have declined substantially in Argentina and Ecuador.

The Social Security Burden

While there are many categories of spending (for example, education, defense, infrastructure, social) among which governments must divide their funds, one of the more worrisome areas is expenditure on social security. In recent years, social security expenditures have become increasingly burdensome. In Argentina, spending on social security as a percentage of total public expenditure has increased dramatically, from 22.4 percent of total public spending in 1980 to 31.3 percent in 1995. In Mexico, social security spending grew to 21.2 percent compared with 13.3 percent while for Brazil the comparable figures are 24.4 percent in 1980 and 33.1 percent in 1994. In Chile, the figure remained relatively constant at 27.3 percent of social spending (see the chart).

Social Security Spending as a Percentage of Total Public Spending

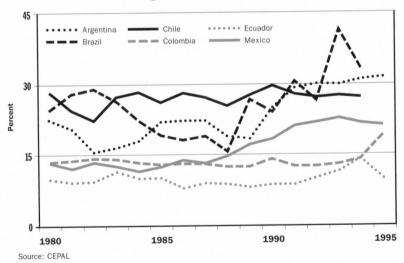

Source: CEPAL

Regionwide, 41 percent of the increase in social spending was due to social security, which is generally considered to be the most regressive area of social spending because social security benefits in Latin America have tended to privilege workers at the higher end of the salary range. In recent years, governments throughout the region have introduced privately managed individual accounts aimed at supplementing or replacing the public pay-as-you-go system. However, funding the transition to private accounts can impose a significant financial burden because governments must continue to fund public systems while workers divert some or all of their payroll tax contributions to individual accounts. Social security reform has engendered considerable political controversy as workers with generous pensions attempt to protect their benefits (Kay 1999).

Conclusion

This article has described in broad strokes the predominant patterns experienced by Latin American countries in managing public sector finance. Literature on this subject suggests that achieving sustainable public sector finance is a multifaceted undertaking. In addition to making sound policy decisions, policymakers are more likely to achieve policy goals when they operate in an institutional setting that is conducive to the successful implementation of these goals. While there has been a consensus for some time among economists about the deleterious impact of prolonged fiscal imbalances, there is a newfound appreciation of the role that institutions play in producing policy outcomes. In short, sustainable public sector finance is neither a purely financial nor a purely institutional and political problem. Rather, the two dimensions of the problem are inextricably intertwined.

The nature of economies in Latin America suggests there is much reason to believe that the region will continue to experience macroeconomic volatility and fluctuating degrees of access to capital markets. Government accounts will continue to reflect this volatility, especially with regard to revenue and interest payments. These factors highlight the need for policymakers to continue pursuing credible economic policy mixes that will balance public sector accounts as well as help to shield the domestic economy from short-term market contagion. Sustainable fiscal policies will help insulate regional economies from greater volatility and smooth out economic swings.

This article has illustrated several specific country experiences as well as examined key patterns on the revenue and expenditure sides of the balance sheet. Some patterns were also noted as countries differentiate themselves in the management of public sector accounts. Future studies will benefit from this diverse set of cases, as well as from improvements in standardized data collection and innovative multidisciplinary approaches.

Notes

1 The authors would like to thank Carlos Lozada and Francisco Parodi for their valuable contributions and excellent research assistance.

2 Gavin and others (1996) and Gavin and Perotti (1997) expanded on these trends.

3 Chile was the only country that posted primary surpluses for the entire ten-year period.

4 Another interesting finding was that fiscal surpluses carry less bang for the buck in Latin American than in industrialized countries. OECD countries get a fiscal stimuli valued around a quarter for every dollar of GDP growth compared with around a nickel in Latin America (Gavin and others 1996, 12–13).

5 Countries subscribing to the Maastricht Treaty are required to keep their public sector external debt below a ratio of no more than 60 percent of GDP. Additionally, budget deficits (that is, the primary deficit) should not be greater than 3 percent of GDP.

6 While several Latin American countries would meet or exceed the 20 percent of external debt service-to-exports ratio set by the World Bank and the IMF for the Highly Indebted Poor Countries initiative, the majority do not qualify for the program because per capita income is higher than the criterion of $925 or less.

Selected Research Bibliography

Além, Ana Cláudia, and Fabio Giambiagi. 1999. "O Ajuste do Governo Central: além das Reformas." In *A Economia Brasileira nos Anos 90*, edited by Fabio Gaimbiagi and Maurício Mesquita Moreira, 86–110. Brasília: Banco Nacional de Desenvolvimento Econômico e Social.

Alesina, Alberto, Ricardo Hausmann, Rudolf Hommes, and Ernesto Stein. 1999. "Budget Institutions and Fiscal Performance in Latin America." *Journal of Development Economics* 59:253–73.

Alesina, Alberto, and Roberto Perotti. 1995. "Fiscal Expansions and Ajustments in OECD Countries." *Economic Policy*, no. 21: 205–48.

Alier, Max, and Martin Kaufman. 1999. "Nonrenewable Resources: A Case for Persistent Fiscal Surpluses." International Monetary Fund Working Paper WP/99/44, April.

Alonso, Julio César, Mauricio Olivera, Israel Fainboim Yaker. 1998. "Sostenibilidad de la política fiscal en América Latina: El caso de Colombia." Inter-American Development Bank, Office of the Chief Economist, Working Paper 319, January.

Arce, Daniel G. 1997. "Fiscal Pacts." *Open economies review* 8, no. 3:271–84.

Arias, Luis A., Elmer Cuba, and Raúl Zalasar. 1997. "La sostenibilidad de la política fiscal en el Perú: 1970–2005." Inter-American Development Bank, Office of the Chief Economist, Working Paper 316, October.

Ball, Laurence, and N. Gregory Mankiw. 1995. "What Do Budget Deficits Do?" In Federal Reserve Bank of Kansas City, 1995. 95–120.

Bates, Robert. 1999. "Institutions and Economic Performance." Paper prepared for delivery at the IMF Conference on Second Generation Reforms, November 8–9.

Bayoumi, Tamim, and Barry Eichengreen. 1994. "Restraining Yourself: Fiscal Rules and Stabilization." International Monetary Fund Working Paper 94/82-EA.

Bevilaqua, Afonso S., and Rogério L.F. Werneck. 1998. "Delaying Public Sector Reforms: Post-Stabilization Fiscal Strains in Brazil." Inter-American Development Bank, Office of the Chief Economist, Working Paper 321, January.

Blanchard, Oliver. 1990. "Suggestions for a New Set of Fiscal Indicators." Organization for Economic Cooperation and Development, Development of Economics and Statistics Working Papers, no. 79, Paris.

Borchardt, Michael, Isabel Rial, and Adolfo Sarmiento. 1998. "Sostenibilidade de la politica fiscal en Uruguay." Inter-American Development Bank, Office of the Chief Economist, Working Paper 320, January.

Bresser Pereira, Luiz Carlos. 1996. *Economic Crisis and State Reform in Brazil: Toward a New Interpretation in Latin America.* Boulder: Lynne Rienner Publishers.

Bresser Pereira, Luiz Carlos, José Maria Maravall, and Adam Przeworski. 1993. *Economic Reforms in New Democracies: A Social-Democratic Approach.* Cambridge: Cambridge University Press.

Cardoso, Fernando Henrique, and Enzo Faletto. 1979. *Dependency and Development in Latin America.* University of California Press.

Cetrangolo, Oscar, Mario Damill, Roberto Frankel, and Juan P. Jimenez. 1998. "La sostenibilidad de la política fiscal en América Latina: El caso argentino." Inter-American Development Bank, Office of the Chief Economist, Working Paper 315.

Chalk, Nigel. 1998. "Fiscal Sustainability and Non-Renewable Resources." International Monetary Fund Working Paper WP/98/26, March.

Chang, Roberto, and Andrés Velasco. 1998. "The Asian Liquidity Crisis." National Bureau of Economic Research Working Paper WP 6796, November.

Chase Securities. 1999. *Chase Emerging Markets Quarterly Outlook.* Second Quarter.

Cominetti, Rosella, and Gonzalo Ruiz. 1998. *Evolución del Gasto Público Social en América Latina: 1980–1995.* Santiago: CEPAL.

Comisión Económica para América Latina y el Caribe (CEPAL). 1999. *Panorama Social de America Latina 1998.* Santiago, CEPAL.

Dahan, Momi. 1998. "The Fiscal Effects of Monetary Policy." International Monetary Fund Working Paper WP/98/66, May.

Daniel, Betty C. 1997. "Fiscal Policy and the Predictability of Exchange Rate Collapse." International Monetary Fund Working Paper WP/97/133, October.

Daniel, James A., Jeffrey M. Davis, and Andrew M. Wolfe. 1997. "Fiscal Accounting of Bank Restructuring." International Monetary Fund Paper on Policy Analysis and Assessment PPAA/97/5, May.

Drudi, Francesco, and Alessandro Prati. 1999. "Signaling Fiscal Regime Sustainability." International Monetary Fund Working Paper WP/99/86, July.

Dwyer, Gerald P., and R.W. Hafer. 1998. "The Federal Government's Budget Surplus: Cause for Celebration?" Federal Reserve Bank of Atlanta *Economic Review* 83 (Third Quarter): 42–51.

Easterly, William, and Sergio Robelo. 1993. "Fiscal Policy and Economic Growth: An Empirical Observation." *Journal of Monetary Economics* no. 32:417–58.

Easterly, William, Carlos Alfredo Rodríguez, and Klaus Schmidt-Hebbel, eds. 1994. *Public Sector Deficits and Macroeconomic Performance.* Oxford: Oxford University Press.

Federal Reserve Bank of Kansas City. 1995. *Budget Deficits and Debt: Issues and Options.* Proceedings from a symposium sponsored by the Federal Reserve Bank of Kansas City in Jackson Hole, Wyoming, August 31–September 2.

Fukuyama, Francis. 1999. "Social Capital and Civil Society." Paper prepared for delivery at the IMF Conference on Second Generation Reforms, November 8–9.

Garcia Osio, Gustavo, Rafael Rodriguez Balza, Luis Marcano, Ricardo Penfold, and Gustavo Sanchez. 1998. "La sostenibilidad de la política fiscal en Venezuela." Inter-American Development Bank, Office of the Chief Economist, Working Paper 317.

Gavin, Michael, Ricardo Hausmann, Roberto Perotti, and Ernesto Talvi. 1996. "Managing Fiscal Policy in Latin America and the Caribbean: Volatility, Procyclicality, and Limited Creditworthiness." Inter-American Development Bank, Office of the Chief Economist, Working Paper 326, March 10.

Gavin, Michael, and Roberto Perotti. 1997. "Fiscal Policy in Latin America." *NBER Macroeconomics Annual 1997.* Cambridge, Mass.: MIT Press.

Haggard, Stephan, and Robert R. Kaufman. 1992. *The Politics of Economic Adjustment.* Princeton: Princeton University Press.

Hart, Albert G. 1970. "Fiscal Policy in Latin America." *Journal of Political Economy* 78 no. 4:857–89.

Hashim, Ali, and Bill Allan. 1994. "Core Functional Requirements for Fiscal Management Systems." International Monetary Fund Working Paper WP/94/27, March.

Hemming, Richard, and James Daniel. 1995. "When Is a Fiscal Surplus Appropriate?" International Monetary Fund Paper on Policy Analysis and Assessment PPAA/95/2, February.

Horne, Jocelyn. 1991. "Indicators of Fiscal Sustainability." International Monetary Fund Working Paper WP/91/5, January.

Inter-American Development Bank. 1997. "Fiscal Stability with Democracy and Decentralization." In *Economic and Social Progress in Latin America: Latin America after a Decade of Reforms.* Washington, D.C.: Inter-American Development Bank, 99–214.

International Monetary Fund. 1999. *World Economic Outlook.* October.

Kalmanovitz, Salomón. 1999. "La política fiscal colombiana en un contexto histórico." Unpublished Paper, January 18.

Kay, Stephen J. 1999. "Unexpected Privatizations: Politics and Social Security Reform in the Southern Cone" *Comparative Politics* 31 no. 4:403–22.

Kopits, George, and Steven Symansky. 1998. "Fiscal Policy Rules." International Monetary Fund Occasional Paper 162.

Lal, Deepak. 1999. "Culture, Democracy, and Development—the Impact of Formal and Informal Institutions on Development." Paper prepared for delivery at the IMF Conference on Second Generation Reforms, November 8–9.

López Murphy, Ricardo. 1995. *Fiscal Decentralization in Latin America*. Baltimore: Johns Hopkins University Press.

Mackenzie, G.A. 1997. "The Macroeconomic Impact of Privatization." International Monetary Fund Paper on Policy Analysis and Assessment 97/9, November.

Mackenzie, G.A., and Peter Stella. 1996. "Quasi-Fiscal Operations of Public Financial Institutions." International Monetary Fund Occasional Paper 142, October.

Mackenzie, G.A., David W.H. Orsmond, and Philip R. Gerson. 1997. "The Composition of Fiscal Adjustment and Growth: Lessons from Fiscal Reforms in Eight Economies." International Monetary Fund Occasional Paper 149, March.

McDermott, C. John, and Robert F. Wescott. 1996. "An Empirical Analysis of Fiscal Adjustments." International Monetary Fund Working Paper WP/96/59, June.

Ministério da Fazenda. Secretaria do Tesouro Nacional. 1998. *Finanças Públicas: II Prêmio STN de Monografia*. Brasília: Government of Brazil.

O'Connor, James. 1973. *The Fiscal Crisis of the State*. New York: St. Martin's Press.

Perry, Guillermo, and Ana María Herrera. 1994. *Public Finances, Stabilization and Structural Reform in Latin America*. Washington, D.C.: Inter-American Development Bank.

Rigolon, Francisco, and Fabio Giambiagi. 1999. "A Renegociação das Dívidas e o Regime Fiscal dos Estados." In *A Economia Brasileira nos Anos 90*, edited by Fabio Gaimbiagi and Maurício Mesquita Moreira. Brasília: Banco Nacional de Desenvolvimento Econômico e Social, 111–44.

Rodrik, Dani. 1999. "Institutions for High-Quality Growth: What They Are and How To Acquire Them." Paper prepared for delivery at the IMF Conference on Second Generation Reforms, November 8–9.

Smith, Willam C., Carlos H. Acuña, and Eduardo A. Gamarra, eds. 1994. *Latin American Political Economy in the Age of Neoliberal Reform: Theoretical and Comparative Perspectives for the 1990s*. Miami: University of Miami North-South Center.

———. 1994. *Democracy, Markets, and Structural Reform in Latin America: Argentina, Bolivia, Brazil, Chile, and Mexico*. Miami: University of Miami North-South Center.

Smith, William C. and Roberto Patricio Korzeniewicz. 1997. *Politics, Social Change, and Economic Restructuring in Latin America*. Boulder: Lynne Rienner Publishers.

Stein, Ernesto, Ernesto Talvi, and Alejandro Grisanti. 1998. *Institutional Arrangements and Fiscal Performance: The Latin American Experience*. NBER Working Paper 6358. Cambridge, MA: National Bureau of Economic Research.

Talvi, Ernesto. 1995. "Fiscal Policy and the Business Cycle Associated with Exchange Rate-Based Stabilizations: Evidence from Uruguay's 1978 and 1991 Programs." Inter-American Development Bank, Office of the Chief Economist, Working Paper 313, November.

Tanzi, Vito. 1990. "Fiscal Issues in Adjustment Programs in Developing Countries." Development Studies Working Paper no. 26 (Turin/Oxford: Centra Studi Luca d'Agliano/Queen Elizabeth House), September. Cited in Ter-Minassian and Schwartz 1997.

———. 1996. "Fiscal Federalism and Decentralization: A Review of Some Efficiency and Macroeconomic Aspects." In *Annual World Bank Conference on Development*

Economics 1995, edited by Michael Bruno and Boris Pleskovic. Washington, D.C: The World Bank.

———. 1999. "The Quality of the Public Sector." Paper prepared for delivery at the IMF Conference on Second Generation Reforms, November 8–9.

Tanzi, Vito, and Howell H. Zee. 1996. "Fiscal Policy and Long-Run Growth." International Monetary Fund Working Paper WP/96/119, October.

Ter-Minassian, Teresa. 1997. "Decentralizing Government." *Finance & Development.* International Monetary Fund, September.

Ter-Minassian, Teresa, and Gerd Schwartz. 1997. "The Role of Fiscal Policy in Sustainable Stabilization: Evidence from Latin America." International Monetary Fund Working Paper WP/97/94, August.

Thomas, Vinod. 1999. "The Quality of Growth." Paper prepared for delivery at the IMF Conference on Second Generation Reforms, November 8–9.

United Nations Economic Commission for Latin America and the Caribbean. 1998. *The Fiscal Covenant: Strengths, Weaknesses, Challenges.* Santiago, Chile.

Wildavsky, Aaron. 1986. *Budgeting: A Comparative Theory of Budgeting Processes.* New Brunswick: Transaction Books.

World Bank. 1999. *Global Development Finance: Country Tables.* Washington, D.C.

Political Constraints on Sustainable Public Sector Development in Latin America

Political Constraints on Sustainable Public Sector Development in Latin America

LAWRENCE S. GRAHAM
University of Texas at Austin

More so than any other recent event, the political changes in Venezuela linked to the election of Hugo Chávez as president in December 1998 call attention to the explosive ramifications of the politics of exclusion that go hand in hand with the revival of markets in Latin America. For the last two decades, economic reforms identified with market-friendly strategies that promote economic stabilization and new economic growth have engendered a debate over their impact on social inequities in the region. The very discourse that has ensued, with its references to redemocratization and neoliberalism, flag the unresolved social and political issues in South America that shape this debate. For, if we stand the hemisphere on its head and survey the region from the vantage point of those countries that first experienced sustained political and economic progress early in this century, beginning with the Southern Cone countries and Brazil, it becomes clearer that for most of the countries in this region, this is not their first encounter with either democracy or markets. Rather, the political and economic history of Latin America, seen from this perspective, involves long-standing experience with the struggle to make democratic institutions work and to make markets perform as an effective way to achieve economic growth and raise the levels of living for all the peoples inhabiting these nations.

What has proven to be endemic for these countries is the repeated breakdown of democratic and market initiatives. Redemocratization speaks to the fact that in South America we have seen distinct cycles of efforts to make democracy work since the nineteenth century, out of which political breakdowns have occurred, leading either to authoritarian rule or major reconfigurations in political power structures. While we do not yet know the outcomes of the current democratic wave, there are signs that political turbulence once again may well constrain or undercut the prospects for further economic and political reforms.

Neoliberalism calls attention to the fact that, despite earlier attempts to install economic liberalism in the late nineteenth and early twentieth centuries and to build national markets, the countries making the greatest progress under that economic model suffered dramatic losses in the late 1920s and early 1930s. Seen from this perspective, the current cycle represents yet another attempt to make markets work and to create appropriate mechanisms for governance to sustain reform initiatives. Thus, this current shift to markets offsets a half-century of experimentation with alternative strategies designed to replace the first model by letting the state assume responsibility for stimulating economic development through state-owned enterprises or joint ventures. State-led economic activity was set up to constrain the earlier reliance on foreign capital and to fill the vacuum where domestic entrepreneurship appeared to be in short supply.

Redemocratization speaks to the fact that these countries have experienced two earlier cycles of democratization, only to experience breakdown and the recursion to authoritarian rule; this failure was due to the inability of limited democracies to respond to demands for substantive democratic reforms made by those excluded from the benefits of earlier economic growth. The issue posed in these instances was that commitment to procedural democracy (through building support for democratic institutions by deciding one's leaders exclusively at the ballot box and by legislating economic and social reforms according to the majority principle) did not create a mechanism through which social and economic inequities could be dealt with effectively; that is, they did not demonstrate to the poor and the excluded that the substance of democracy, measured in terms of equality of opportunity, could attend to their desires to improve their socioeconomic conditions.

Given the diversity of the political and economic experiences of the Latin American states, an effective way to capture both the political constraints that are emerging in the present, as well as the paths pursued in the past that continue to shape the present, is to use theoretically relevant case studies. By examining key country cases that flag developments that later became crucial in the evolution of politics and economics in the region, it becomes easier to understand the continuing political and social forces that have the capacity to constrain or reverse the shift toward markets. To capture these developments, Argentina, Brazil, Mexico, and Venezuela are particularly relevant.

The Argentine Case: Harnessing Populism to Fit the Demands of Neoliberalism

In the debate over which political and economic models are most appropriate for achieving sustained economic growth while also installing political regimes responsive to the values of progress and individual freedom transferred into the New World from Western Europe, no country in the region demonstrates more effectively than Argentina the ties between the past and the present. In the first wave of economic and political reforms in the Americas, the commitment to late nineteenth-century economic liberalism and political democracy in Argentina moved that country to the forefront of the Latin American republics. On the eve of the Great Depression of 1929, Argentines could look back on forty years of spectacular growth and development that put their country at the threshold of a future on a par with the economic and political achievements identified with Western Europe. Through external investments (especially British), massive European immigration, commercialization of its agricultural resources in beef and wheat, and commitment to procedural democracy through electoral reform (for example, through the Saenz Peña Act of 1912), Argentina's leaders had created a vibrant economy and a political democracy in which universal male suffrage had become accepted. Elections were generally agreed upon as the appropriate mechanism through which national leaders could be selected to govern.

For all its successes, however, the prevailing economic and political regime was not without its problems. Labor protest in urban and rural areas in the late 1910s and early 1920s signaled the fact that while the new middle classes were able to integrate themselves effectively into a growing economy and expanding political system, working-class individuals found little tolerance for reallocating economic resources in a way that permitted higher wages or for changing the bases of political power to allow adjustments in social benefits to those disadvantaged by the shifts in the economy in urban and rural areas. Consequently, when generalized economic collapse hit the country in 1929, those who had the power to impose an immediate solution closed the political system down in order to control social unrest, ensure order, and give priority to economic recovery. Fifteen years later, in the context of World War II, neither full economic nor political recovery had been achieved. What did occur was that, after more than a decade of attempted economic and political engineering, a group of younger military officers with lower-middle-class backgrounds carried out a more radical coup within the earlier coup of their military superiors. One of these officers, Colonel Juan Perón, who was assigned to be Minister of Labor, found a working-class constituency responsive to his attempts to attend to their needs and willing to accept his leadership to achieve immediate economic and social revindication. Despite the attempts of military superiors to sideline him, when he and his wife Evita fought back, they found a huge mass of working-class men and women backing them and willing to go into the streets to support them. In a very short period of time, the Peróns discovered a huge popular mandate supporting them, and they were able to convert this support into a new political movement that overwhelmed existing civilian and military forces.

Consolidated in the election of 1946, Peronismo introduced a new, popularly based, mass political movement that changed Argentine politics and economics once and for all, through suspending the rules of procedural democracy and imposing by force what the masses perceived to be substantive democratic gains. By enfranchising workers, not so much through formal politics as through guaranteeing immediate economic and social benefits that adjusted disparities in income and in access to social services, the Peróns built what their supporters believed to be a social justice movement. The Movimiento Justicialista guaranteed immediate and direct substantive gains for working-class Argentines under progressively more and more authoritarian practices, in the name of direct and substantive adjustments in social and economic inequities. For this reason, when we speak of populism in the Latin American context, the Argentine experience frequently becomes the prototype of the populist movements that swept across the region in the 1940s and the 1950s and into the 1960s. Rejecting disciplined political party organizations, mass movements rallying behind middle-class leaders dominated the second wave of democracy that followed the end of World War II.

In a second wave of democratic experimentation, limited democracies followed these earlier democratic breakdowns, characterized by populist authoritarian governments or restricted right-wing authoritarian regimes. No stable form of democratic rule could be found in these limited democracies because the dominant political and military rulers were determined to exclude or to limit populist forces through writing democratic rules that constrained the impact of the masses. Each of the countries experiencing this second phase of democratic rule has a distinct set of national experiences. Once again, however, the Argentine case further defines this prototype in that it directed attention to the creation of populist democracies and the attempt to sustain democratic regimes, as long as they did not threaten the political and economic power of national elites.

Argentina's reencounter with democratic rule under these conditions extends from 1958 to 1966, followed by a long cycle of authoritarian rule, from 1966 to 1984, broken intermittently by failed attempts to reestablish democracy. The breakdown of this second democratic cycle, which provided for much less stable democratic practices, generated a longer cycle of authoritarianism. Failed initiatives to return power to civilians ultimately led to violence and made hard-line military authorities determined to repress opposition at all costs. On the economic side, throughout these years an alternative economic model—import-substitution-industrialization—prevailed; the state also practiced active involvement in the economy to control markets and exchange rates and sought to stimulate new economic development through joint ventures or state-owned enterprises.

Both of these political and economic reform initiatives eventually failed. In the shifts in Argentine politics since January 1984, the two major political movements, the Radicales and the Peronistas, laid aside their differences and recognized the desirability of a redemocratized polity in which both could compete openly at the ballot box. Once the Peronistas, under the leadership of their new leader Carlos Menem, were able to demonstrate a clear-cut popular majority and to gain power, major economic restructuring followed. Import-substitution-industrialization and state-dominated economic policies were replaced by rapid movement in the direction of free markets under neoliberal economic policies. These policies first emphasized fiscal stabilization and then significant structural adjustments to ensure the functioning of market mechanisms without constraints. In the Argentine setting this accomplishment was made possible by Menem's ability to refocus the forces of populism in his society in such a way as to put together a dominant coalition that extended across two terms of office. In the process, Peronismo was redefined as Menemismo: the techniques of power for obtaining mass support first developed by the Peróns were reformulated and converted into a new populist coalition that supported the dramatic turnaround in the Argentine economy.

While there were important variations in this resurgence of populism elsewhere in Latin America during the 1990s, Argentina once again has become the prototype of what is now called neopopulism. The term refers to the use of populist political practices in a democratic context to enlist mass political support for the purposes of economic restructuring. These refurbished mass movements have been reconfigured to fit the times, principally through redefining the link between leader and working-class and lower-middle-class support. Neopopulist leaders advocate (1) abandoning statism, (2) refocusing nationalism by reaffirming confidence in one's own society in cooperation with the new economic forces identified with globalization, and (3) heightening the powers of the presidency by minimizing the impact of parties, legislatures, and the courts under presidentialist forms of governance (Roberts 1995; Weyland 1996).[1]

The Brazilian Case: Reform-Mongering while Encouraging Democratic Practices

Yet another emerging pattern of political constraints on sustainable public sector development in Latin America can be illustrated by looking at Brazil. There the path taken diverges from the Argentine example in that the new political economy, with its emphasis on markets, democracy, and institutional reform under the presidency of Fernando Henrique Cardoso, converges with the decision to follow a political model emphasizing decentralization and engineering economic and political reforms that respect the principle of the division of powers inherent in democratic presidential practices. Throughout his rule Cardoso has accepted consistently the limits placed on the presidency by Congress and the courts and has attempted to sustain a strategy of economic and political reform by working within these constraints, thus promoting democratic initiatives in Brazil.

During these years, the government (that is, the two administrations of Fernando Henrique Cardoso, from 1995 to 1998 and from 1999 to 2002), has followed the new orthodoxy in structural reform. First, it achieved economic stabilization through the Plano *Real*. Then it undertook an aggressive privatization program that involved a political reform component, amending the constitution in those areas where public enterprise has been linked most closely with economic nationalism. Subsequently, once Cardoso had engineered his reelection for a second term of office, the government expanded the scope of its political reforms by increasing the powers of the federal government in fiscal policy; it did so, however, at the expense of the state governments through the imposition of federal controls over state indebtedness. The devaluation of the *real* on January 13, 1999, the decision to float the country's currency on January 15, and the acceptance of a de facto loss in the value of the *real*, which mounted initially to approximately 40 percent, produced economic turbulence. By the second half of the year the exchange rate was fluctuating between 1.8 and 1.9 *reais* to the dollar. Within this context, the image of Cardoso as an effective leader quickly moved from positive assessments in the polls to increasingly negative reactions in the drift of Brazilian politics as Cardoso ran into more and more opposition in Congress. Overnight an image of stalemate and stasis at the national level replaced the earlier one of reform and change.

In this setting, the reformist strategy Cardoso had used so successfully in his first administration became the source of his difficulties in the second. Earlier, to achieve the constitutional reforms necessary to sustain his commitment to privatization, Cardoso had built and maintained a broad-based coalition that brought together reformers and moderates on the center-right. Key to this coalition was an alliance among his own party, the Brazilian Social Democratic Party (the PSDB), the Party of the Brazilian Democratic Movement (the PMDB), and the Liberal Front Party (the PFL). To this one should add a number of smaller parties and representatives in Congress, who were also rallied to muster the three-fifths votes needed in each house, in two successive votes in each chamber, to reform the constitution.

As Cardoso moved into his second term, he faced major difficulties. Already the criticism had been levied against his government that, in the commitment to markets and extensive privatization, there was no place for social reform. As the new budget took form, it was clear that there would be even larger cuts in health, education, and social welfare. When all this settled out, by July 1999, major splits within the government and problems with the administration's coalition in Congress produced an alliance that was notably farther to the right. The alliance was more dependent than ever on the support of the PFL and its leader, Antônio Carlos Magalhães. The immediate cause of this shift was political reality. While the coalition supporting Cardoso in Congress consisted largely of the same parties, electoral outcomes produced an important realignment. In the new congress, the conservative PFL led by Magalhães had the largest number of representatives, followed by the PMDB, whose centrist position produced more ambiguity than ever. In third place was Cardoso's PSDB with Michel Temer as president of the Chamber of Deputies. The coherency of the PFL organization and Magalhães's leadership role in that party as president of the senate, combined with the coalition character of the PSDB and the PMDB, meant that Magalhães had become an even more important player in national politics in Cardoso's second administration. The net result was Cardoso's increasing dependence on Magalhães for any legislation he wished to pass and the limiting of his options at best to economic measures. In that setting, negotiating further reforms ceased to be a viable option.

While Cardoso's commitment to economic and political reforms within the framework of democratic politics was notable during his first administration, his difficulties in sustaining reform initiatives in his second administration calls attention to the limits of "reform-mongering" in democratic Brazil.[2] Increasingly, lacking a majority in Congress to support further economic reform initiatives, he has had to opt for a strategy in which further economic structuring has been occurring by default, allowing market forces to determine economic outcomes.[3] Herein lies the anomaly of an economy that continues to do well, despite increased unemployment and economic dislocations, both of which are linked to protests and demonstrations against the economic changes under way.

The Mexican Case: Engineering State Reform in the Midst of Democratization

Mexican developments highlight yet another path taken in engineering political, economic, and institutional reform in today's Latin America. The redefinition of the role of the state throughout Latin America over the last decade cannot be separated from the realm of politics or from the economic and political transitions that have swept across the hemisphere. The side of the equation that is probably best understood falls within the purview of economics: the return to markets as the primary regulating force has led to a retreat of the state from intervention in the economy. On a worldwide basis, state shrinking is a consequence of structural adjustment policies—those policies that require major changes in the structure of the economy, the state, and society. In Latin America, the most visible aspects of this change to date have been the use of monetary policy to end inflation; the recourse to privatization; and the opening up of national economies, previously dominated by state-owned enterprises and statist strategies for economic growth, to private sector firms. What has been much more difficult to achieve is structural change within the apparatus of the state itself. Here the case of Mexico is instructive for understanding how difficult it is to move from the first phase of structural adjustment policies into the second, in which restructuring of political and administrative institutions is required to consolidate markets. If Brazil illustrates the limits of political reform while attempting to enhance democracy and markets, Mexico speaks to the difficulties of reforming the state while attempting simultaneously to restructure the economy and to democratize.

The issue of state reform has been a major part of the policy agendas of Mexican presidents since the six-year term of office, or the *sexenio*, of José López Portillo, which ran from 1976 to 1982. Because these attempts at state reform stretch across more than twenty years, engaging major economic and political change in the process, the tension there between sweeping internal political and economic changes and external conditionalities identified with structural adjustment policies is the greatest. Yet, despite long-standing debates over the direction the Mexican transition is taking as well as competition between government and the opposition to control the process, economic reform coupled with administrative reform has continued inside the government. Regardless of differences over the direction and the content of the political opening, both sides generally have concurred that continued progress in economic reform is contingent on extensive changes in the state's administrative apparatus. While calls for administrative reform are not new to Mexico, what is different about current discussions is the extent to which economic reform has become linked to administrative reform. As a consequence, a new consensus has emerged between the Mexican business community and central-government officials that civil service reform—emphasizing nonpartisan, merit-oriented criteria in recruitment and promotion—is in their best interest. This is especially the case when one compares the programs of Partido de Acción Nacional (PAN), the leading opposition party, in the states and major cities where it now holds office with those of President Ernesto Zedillo and his Partido Revolucionario Institucional (PRI) in the federal bureaucracy.

This convergence between reformers in both camps must be juxtaposed against increasing turbulence and uncertainty in politics as the pace of change accelerates in Mexican society. There is a simple reason why this is the case. For all the problems and difficulties inherent in the present situation, Mexico continues to have a relatively strong state, in which public officials in strategic sectors have considerable capacity to design and to implement the economic and social policies to which government is committed. Groups in the center and on the right politically do not wish to see this resource squandered. In this regard, Mexican experience in state building stands in marked contrast with that of most other developing countries; in Latin America only Chile can match the Mexican record.

In the eyes of Mexican reformers, a technocratic revolution is under way. While set back by unexpected political assassinations, popular protests and revolts, and continued instances of police corruption, those operating inside the federal government have not lessened in the least their push to consolidate a new regime based on the instrumentalities of a strong state. For example, those identified with what is often referred to as the New PRI, a new alliance between professionals and party officials committed to greater transparency in politics but not in government, differ little from those staffing PAN governments in the city of Monterrey and the state government of Nuevo León. Furthermore, Miguel Ángel Centeno, the author of an important book on the internal workings of the Mexican state, argues that when one looks at the top, and examines elite interaction, separation between party (the PRI) and government has already occurred (Centeno 1994).[4]

Against the desiderata of these reformers must be juxtaposed more than a half-century of partisan political practices. Reformers, operating at the apex of the political and economic systems, have the capacity to shape policy and control the reform agenda, and they wish to expand that capacity. But their success in determining macroeconomic policy does not translate into an ability to implement other aspects of economic and social policy at the grassroots level. For all the talk of reform, the issue of corruption and influence peddling abounds at the state and local levels. Seen from below, within the middle and lower levels of government employees, and outside government in the middle and working sectors of society, the labels of party and government remain inseparable. From this perspective, one of the major challenges at the end of the Zedillo *sexenio* concerns whether or not it will be possible to move this debate among insiders over reform of the state out of the offices of the privileged and into mass-based state and party organizations without rupturing the prevailing presidentialist regime. As Centeno makes so clear in his analysis of the technocratic revolution in Mexico, the past strength of the PRI party state was its ability to sustain a political settlement in which the civilian bureaucracy was able to retain the upper hand over politicians and the military, within the framework of a single dominant party organization that could deliver mass support (47–51).

As pressures have increased for adjustments in social policy to absorb the further dislocations likely to occur as economic liberalization advances, the old formula of bureaucratic expertise at the top and political party patronage below within the organs of the state can no longer work. This is because along with greater transparency in the economy has come greater transparency in politics. In the older political world controlled by the PRI, public employment at the middle and lower levels of

Mexican society was linked to job creation and enhancement for individuals who lacked employment opportunities elsewhere in the economy. This style of political clientelism is no longer compatible either with the newer demands for greater efficiency and effectiveness in government as the economic reforms advance or with the opening up of politics in such a way that more and more government officials are finding themselves subject to public scrutiny and accountable for their actions.

The impact of the North American Free Trade Agreement (NAFTA) and of sustained support for this agreement in Mexico among elites, despite economic hardship for major segments of the Mexican population, argue for a state at the middle and upper levels that is less politicized than conventional wisdom would suggest. Thus, when this administrative equation is added to the revolt in Chiapas and the PRI's loss of Nuevo León and its capital, Monterrey, it is not so clear that the Mexican transition is necessarily linked to continued democratization. These components call attention to the fact that, while the movement away from old-style authoritarianism is irreversible, it is not at all certain that greater transparency in the economy will automatically generate greater transparency in government and hence lead to democratic consolidation. Quasifederalist experiments characteristic of Mexican governance since the late 1970s may well become the foundation for a quasidemocratic regime in the 1990s that extends beyond the year 2000. This regime would be characterized by a strong state in the center identified with a new PRI in control of the presidency, greater respect for electoral majorities, and greater political competition—but without necessarily bringing an end to PRI dominance of national politics.

The alternative emerging in Mexico is not so much a retreat of the state in the administrative field; it is rather a movement from an era in which groups struggled to control the state and build new forms of state power into one in which a weak state is dominated by interests and groups in society that are pulverizing the state, thus increasing its incoherence and its marginality as a force attending to social policy. What is under way is not just privatization in the economy but privatization of social policy: social security systems, educational establishments, health systems, and other social institutions, which in an earlier era were brought into the domain of the state, are now being cut loose and moved into an environment characterized by competing social and political groups engaged in a struggle to determine who will design and control the policies that will determine the nature of the projects and the programs to be pursued. Here the case of Venezuela becomes as important as the experiences of

Argentina, Brazil, and Mexico, as long as we keep in mind that retaining a relatively strong state, as is the case with Mexico and Chile, defines a path very different from neopopulism and reform-mongering in a democratic environment tied to presidentialism.

The Venezuelan Case: Resurgence of Old-Style Populism

From 1958 through 1998 the progress made in institutionalizing democratic practices in Venezuela was impressive. An earlier pattern of confrontation politics had culminated with Acción Democrática (AD) demonstrating its capacity to obtain an absolute majority in national elections in 1946, only to trigger a military coup in 1948 and dictatorship under General Marcos Pérez Jiménez (from 1952 to 1958), thus reversing what were perceived to be radical reforms. Seeking an end to this pattern of reversals, the leaders of the three major parties—the majoritarian AD, the Christian Democrats or COPEI as the leading opposition party, and a smaller populist party, the Unión Radical Democrática made up of AD dissidents— banded together in a political pact. In the Pacto de Punto Fijo they committed themselves to respecting electoral outcomes as the sole legitimate way to determine the country's government. Eschewing taking power by alternative means and agreeing to respect the norms of procedural democracy, they proceeded to institutionalize democratic practices. Facilitating this agreement was Venezuela's newfound oil wealth, which from the 1930s onward made the country one of the major oil-producing countries and produced steadily increasing governmental revenues. Yet, agreement on democratic rules was not easily accomplished. First, AD and its opponents had to make democracy work by getting their leaders and followers to respect electoral outcomes, when that meant turning over government to one's opponents under conditions of extreme partisanship. As a left-of-center political movement mobilizing workers in the oil industry, in the cities and countryside, AD had to convince its political allies that they could use their electoral majorities to govern effectively. They accomplished this objective by designing and implementing a reform agenda that would respect the reservations of their political opponents in the center and the right while fighting a guerrilla movement on the left that sought revolutionary changes. In the process, AD modified its agenda, became increasingly a centrist political alliance, and benefited from the left's eventual abandonment of armed struggle and acceptance of the principle of competition at the ballot box. When, after two terms of office, AD lost national elections to COPEI in 1968, it was not at all certain that its left wing would honor the commitment to accept the transfer of power to a party of center-right Christian Democrats in 1969. Party splits resulted, but AD's Rómulo Betancourt remained adamant they would pass into the opposition. In an electoral system marked by repeated scandals, charges of corruption, and accusations of manipulated results in electoral districts, the party leadership on both sides honored the agreement. What ensued was a succession of party governments in which AD and COPEI, as the two major parties, alternated in office for the next twenty-five years. In the process, the country passed through partial agrarian reform, gradual nationalization of the oil industry, and alternative economic programs designed to lessen dependency on oil and to stimulate national economic development.

Throughout these years, there was a continuing debate among political analysts about the basis of the country's success in sustaining commitment to democratic rule, despite initial conditions of adversity, the split between right and left over the country's future, and AD's commitment to finding a middle way. Critics argued that what sustained Venezuelan democracy was its oil-based economy, which subsidized government and made it possible to use the country's economic wealth and oil revenues to ameliorate social and economic conditions by rewarding the party faithful with subsidies, jobs, and direct benefits. Others defended the accomplishments by pointing out how consensus had been built on democratic rules, how the revolutionary left had been isolated, defeated, and then folded into the system, and how the country was making progress in diversifying its economy and laying a foundation for sustained economic progress.[5]

Then, in 1989 economic crisis hit Venezuela in a way that transformed the country's economy and politics. In February 1989 riots broke out against austerity measures designed to correct the country's economic decline as oil revenues dropped precipitously. AD's Carlos Andrés Pérez, in office for a second term after an earlier presidency from 1974 to 1979, responded with policies intended to balance the necessary economic restructuring under austerity measures and neoliberal reforms with a continuation of the social subsidies and party favoritism that had long characterized Venezuela's democracy. Economic and political turbulence increased, however, rather than lessened. The economic situation continued to deteriorate, leading to a virtual collapse of the banking system in 1994, followed by a $9 billion international bailout. Political partisanship reached unprecedented levels as one political scandal followed another and Carlos Andrés Pérez's involvement became more and more murky.

This culminated in two failed military coups in 1992 to remove him by force from office, his impeachment by Congress in May 1993, and his removal from office in such a way that, while AD suffered the brunt of the criticism, COPEI was equally damaged. In the subsequent presidential election, COPEI's Rafael Caldera found it necessary to stand as the head of a multiparty coalition minimizing his ties with his own party. But Caldera too failed to resolve the country's economic crisis. Then, in December 1998, voter revolt against the established parties generated a clear-cut victory for one of the former coup leaders, Hugo Chávez. Convinced that he had a mandate from the voters, Chávez imposed radical change by altering the country's political system and convoking elections in July 1999 for a constituent assembly to write a new constitution. He attacked Congress (where the opposition retained a majority) and the courts for opposing his implementation of what he perceived to be a mandate from the voters to change prevailing political and economic policies radically by concentrating power in the Office of the Presidency.

This political explosion in Venezuela, first in the December 1998 election of Chávez by a clear majority, then by constituent assembly elections with an even higher level of support in July 1999, and followed by a favorable standing in the polls of an estimated 75 percent in September, signaled the return of old-style populism with a vengeance. This mass movement of the disenfranchised and the excluded demanded immediate social justice and a redistribution of the nation's wealth to benefit the majority. The classic ingredients originally present in Juan and Evita Perón's Movimiento Justicialista have thus been galvanized in a way not seen since the late 1940s and early 1950s in Argentina: charismatic leadership, mass political support breaking with previous party and political structures, and revindication in the demand for direct and substantive economic and social benefits for the popular masses. While parallels can be identified with the policies of Carlos Menem in Argentina, Alberto Fujimori in Peru, and Hugo Banzer in Bolivia, this is not neopopulism in the way those countries' leaders harnessed populism as a mass movement to legitimize neoliberal economic reforms. Rather, the Venezuelan upheaval has all the ingredients identified with the political explosion in Argentina of the 1940s, which ruptured that country's politics and economics in such a way that it took fifty years to reach a new political and economic accommodation. Chávez's demands are for social revindication for the poor and reversal of economic policies identified with austerity measures, externally imposed market reforms, and structural adjustment policies intended to reduce the role of the state in the economy and consolidate markets.

The actions taken by Chávez and his supporters have ruptured the existing framework for democratic politics and thus have set the country on a course in which creating new institutional arrangements within Venezuela, while simultaneously renegotiating economic accords abroad and getting the economy back on track, have proven to be very difficult.[6]

Conclusions and Trends

What the outcomes will be within the Latin American region remains unclear as we move into the next millennium. But the paths and the choices are increasingly clear (see Table 1):

- Neopopulism, in which mass movements outside the framework of established parties can be harnessed to neoliberal economic policies, centers on excesses in presidential power and comes at the expense of constrained democratic practices and limited response to social and economic grievances (the case of Argentina, and the variants present in Peru and Bolivia).
- Reform-mongering in economics and politics is tied to strengthening democratic rule but makes it difficult to achieve economic reforms that require major political and economic restructuring and to respond to social inequities (the case of Brazil and attempts at reform-mongering in such different countries as Chile, since 1989, and Uruguay).
- Advancement of state reform in the midst of democratic initiatives responds to demands for opening up participation and contestation in society, after the initial restructuring of the economy and the state under authoritarianism (the cases of Mexico and Chile, before 1989, with the understanding that the inclusionary authoritarian system of the former and the exclusionary one of the latter produced very different reform policies and outcomes once the decision to democratize was made).
- Reversion to old-style populism increases economic and political turbulence and has a negative impact both on markets and politics insofar as the survival of substantive democratic practices is concerned (the recent experiences of Venezuela and Ecuador).

Nevertheless, identification of these four paths in Latin America in response to global pressures to move to markets should not be taken to

TABLE 1: **Responses to Neoliberalism in Latin America: The Four Major Alternatives**	
Neopopulism	Argentina, Peru, Bolivia
Reform-Mongering	Brazil, Uruguay, Chile (since 1989)
State Reform	Mexico, Chile (before 1989)
Old-Style Populism	Venezuela, Ecuador

exclude the possibility that new hybrid patterns might evolve. Just as the study of Argentina's experience with old and new forms of populism identifies a path in which there are significant new developments in Bolivia and Peru, so too there are variants in the path taken by Brazil in its reformist policies that account for very different outcomes in Chilean and Uruguayan politics today. Likewise, it is not at all certain that the breakthrough of the excluded masses in Venezuela in a way similar to Peronismo will produce a radical break with the neoliberal economic policies dominant in Latin America. The argument can be made that the current coalition of international forces favoring free markets may well place such constraints on Chávez that his leadership will produce yet another variant of neopopulism. Furthermore, while the four paths taken in response to neoliberalism and the country prototypes selected call attention to the diversity of national responses within the region, this should not lead to the conclusion that these are the only patterns. For example, narco-trafficking and guerrilla activity have produced very different outcomes in Colombia. The presence of a consolidated national state system in Latin America means precisely that different responses to globalization will continue to occur as these countries respond to very different sets of domestic and international concerns.

Notes

1   While scholars who call attention to the phenomenon of hyperpresidentialism do not necessarily link this phenomenon to neopopulism, this was an important ingredient in the reappearance of populism in the 1990s. See also Nino (1996).

2   The term reform-mongering was first used by Hirschman (1973) to call attention to the prospects for democratic reforms in the Latin American context, especially during the administration of Eduardo Frei in Chile, when the Christian Democrats controlled the presidency and held a working majority in Congress.

3   The disarray in Cardoso's political coalition should not lead one to conclude that economic restructuring has ceased. To the contrary, strategic planning within the context

of Cardoso's economic team during the first administration already had identified four global scenarios to which the country would have to respond regardless of political outcomes within the country. In the Brazil 2020 project, mounted by the Center for Strategic Studies in the Presidency of the Republic, the National Bank for Economic and Social Development (BNDES), and the Planning Ministry, four scenarios were developed. The two identified as the most relevant to Brazil's immediate economic positioning in the international context were the need to respond to globalization as a process driven essentially by international market forces and the shift toward knowledge-based industries centered on high technology. By the end of 1998 it appeared that Brazil was well situated in the South American context through the Cardoso reforms at the center and the push toward decentralization that had given new meaning to state and local governments to be able to accommodate further economic restructuring through market-based solutions over the short term. While secondary, but of potentially growing importance in individual states and Brazil's more advanced regional economies, the options opening up in the area of knowledge-based industries likewise point to developments at the state and local level that, when combined with state-based economic and political reforms, offset the tensions present in Brasília. See Graham (1999).

4   See especially Chapter 5, "The Technocratic Vanguard."

5   In the extensive literature on Venezuela's democracy, books and articles that capture this debate well are Karl (1986), Levine (1978), Tugwell (1975), and Coppedge (1994).

6   An article indicating that, while Venezuela is at the crossroads in terms of its democratic system, there is still the possibility that this political revolt can be folded into its democratic institutional framework for resolving conflict is "Supporters of a Drive to Reshape Venezuela Make a Retreat: A Constitutional Assembly Is Stung by Criticism," *New York Times*, September 11, 1999, p. A2. Should Venezuela ride out this economic and political crisis of major import, then it will have met a key requirement in passing from what I would define as a democratic situation of long-standing into the ranks of a consolidated democracy. In the current setting, international factors, involving the role of multilateral institutions and the policy options pursued in negotiating economic accords, carry the prospect of avoiding the confrontational politics nationally and internationally that led to the consolidation of a populist mass movement in Argentina and the rupturing of prior political and economic institutions earlier.

References

Centeno, Miguel Angel. 1994. *Democracy within Reason: Technocratic Revolution in Mexico*. University Park: Pennsylvania State University Press.

Coppedge, Michael. 1994. "Venezuela: Democratic Despite Presidentialism." In *The Failure of Presidential Democracy*, edited by Juan J. Linz and Arturo Valenzuela. Baltimore, MD: Johns Hopkins University Press.

Graham, Lawrence S. 1999. "New Dynamics in Economic Restructuring: Cross-National Patterns in Regional Accommodation and the Brazilian Response." Paper prepared for the Third International Conference on Technology Policy and Innovation, Austin, Texas, LBJ School of Public Affairs, August 30–September 2.

Hirschman, Alberto O. 1973. *Journeys Toward Progress: Studies of Economic Policy-Making in Latin America*. New York: Norton.

Karl, Terry Lynn. 1986. "Petroleum and Political Pacts: The Transition to Democracy in Venezuela." In *Transitions from Authoritarian Rule,* edited by Guillermo O'Donnell, Philippe C. Schmitter, and Laurence Whitehead. Baltimore, MD: Johns Hopkins University Press.

Levine, Daniel. 1978. "Venezuela since 1958: The Consolidation of Democratic Politics." In *The Breakdown of Democratic Regimes*, edited by Juan J. Linz and Alfred Stepan. Baltimore, MD: Johns Hopkins University Press.

Nino, Carlos Santiago. 1996. "Hyperpresidentialism and Constitutional Reform in Argentina." In *Institutional Design in New Democracies: Eastern Europe and Latin America,* edited by Arend Lijphart and Carlos H. Waisman. Boulder, CO: Westview Press.

Roberts, Kenneth. 1995. "Neoliberalism and the Transformation of Populism in Latin America: The Peruvian Case." *World Politics* 48 (October).

Tugwell, Franklin. 1975. *The Politics of Oil in Venezuela.* Stanford, CA: Stanford University Press.

Weyland, Kurt. 1996. "Neopopulism and Neoliberalism in Latin America: Unexpected Affinities." *Studies in International Comparative Development* 31 (Fall): 3.

Comments

KURT WEYLAND
Vanderbilt University

Professor Graham's excellent paper provides a wealth of insights and interesting arguments about threats to the political sustainability of Latin America's new market systems. Given my limited time, I want to comment on five of his most important points: the considerable cross-country variation in the processes and outcomes of market reform; the need to enhance state capacity in order to make markets work right; the importance of social policies for keeping the new market systems politically viable; the dangers of a traditional-populist backlash against market reforms and, perhaps, democracy; and the general question of the survival of democracy and its compatibility with a market system.

One of the most important contributions of Professor Graham's paper is his emphasis on and careful analysis of the great variation in the processes and outcomes of "neoliberalism" in Latin America. The processes of market reform differed, ranging from top-down imposition in Peru to negotiation in Brazil. The outcomes of market reform also differ: Argentina and Peru instituted much more radical versions of neoliberalism than Brazil. Since the "neoliberal revolution" in Latin America has not had the same endpoint, the conditions for the political sustainability of the new market system also differ considerably across countries.

These cross-country differences stem partly from long-standing institutional developments, as Professor Graham convincingly demonstrates. This path dependence suggests that markets are always conditioned by their institutional contexts. Specifically, effective state institutions are crucial for making markets work. Public sector reform is therefore very important. By stressing this point, Professor Graham shows that the "orthodox paradox" noted by Miles Kahler is not a transitional issue, but a permanent one (1990, 55). Kahler argued that, paradoxically, the main agent of market reform and state retrenchment must be the state itself. But the need for an effective state exists not only during the process of market reform but also after the market system has been instituted. For instance, it is crucial to have effective governmental regulation of privatized enterprises, reliable guarantees of property rights, an efficient judiciary, and so forth.

In the area of state reform, Latin America confronts two important problems. First, states have too little autonomy from private sector groups. There is too much collusion, and too little transparency and control. This problem becomes evident in the frequent corruption scandals and also in the relaxation of extractive efforts. An important part of the neoliberal package was a recuperation of taxation, which included unprecedented efforts to crack down on tax evasion, especially in Argentina and Peru. But in the last few years, these efforts have weakened, tax evasion has grown again, and fiscal problems have intensified. Thus, there has been some backsliding on fiscal issues that results from diminished state autonomy and that in turn weakens the public sector.

The second problem is states' low capacity for policy implementation, which results from the clientelist machinations stressed by Professor Graham. Another contributing factor is the exodus of qualified personnel, which was exacerbated by neoliberal austerity measures such as salary compression. Furthermore, there are technical difficulties in designing performance-enhancing reforms, as the sobering experiences of Chile in the 1990s suggest. The Aylwin and Frei governments substantially increased public sector salaries, but with little effect on performance. Frei then introduced incentives for greater "productivity," but those are difficult to define and implement. Clearly defined incentives may have perverse consequences: for example, measuring the productivity of a surgeon by the number of operations she performs may stimulate an explosion of unnecessary surgeries. By contrast, more qualitative performance evaluations by superiors keep the door open for clientelism and political manipulation. So, in addition to the political difficulties correctly stressed by Professor Graham, there are also serious technical problems that hinder state reform. Even when there is political will to reform the state, the task is exceedingly complicated.

State performance is usually weakest in the social sectors, which have always been misused for political patronage. The contribution of social policy to alleviating poverty is therefore woefully low, even in countries that engage in substantial social spending, such as Brazil. For this reason, social policy reform is imperative. In fact, market reforms often included innovative social programs that were designed to avoid or remedy some of these problems, especially through the targeting of benefits to the very poor and through demand-driven decision-making procedures. To what extent these new antipoverty programs have been effective remains to be investigated in a thorough and systematic fashion. But some of these programs—for instance, in Peru—did for the first time provide benefits to the urban and especially rural poor who had previously been neglected completely. So there have been some initiatives in this area.

Nevertheless, I fully agree with Professor Graham's call for much greater attention to the tremendous social problems created—or at least not resolved—by market reforms. But I am not sure whether more effective social programs would greatly enhance *political* support for market reforms. This skepticism is inspired by the Chilean case: the Aylwin and Frei governments increased social spending enormously and seriously sought to improve social policies; in fact, poverty diminished considerably in the 1990s. Nevertheless, there is a widespread sense of malaise in Chile. If we can trust opinion surveys, popular support for the principles and realities of the new market system is surprisingly low. So even if social policies improved in other countries, I am not sure whether political backing for the new market system would solidify.

Where social policies do not improve, could festering social discontent threaten the new market system with a traditional-populist backlash, as in present-day Venezuela? Here, I see less of a risk than Professor Graham does. In most countries, the market system has some strong supporters, and even people who do not really like it acquiesce in it, for several reasons. For instance, international pressures and constraints make a reversal very costly. Domestically, many of the losers have diminishing socioeconomic clout and political influence; for instance, business sectors that cannot withstand foreign competition go bankrupt or sell to foreign investors and thus lose control over their main resource, investment capital. By contrast, winning sectors expand and gain greater political weight. Furthermore, the transitional costs of market reform hinder a reversal. They constitute a sunk "investment" that seems to induce many people to give the new market system a try and reject another round of risky experimentation. Obviously, the absence of a global, realistic alternative to the market system also favors its continued predominance. For all of these reasons, I do not see a high risk of reform reversal or traditional-populist backlash.

In fact, the great variation among country experiences that Professor Graham stresses makes a wave of reform reversals unlikely. The resurgence of traditional populism in Venezuela has very specific Venezuelan roots. This backlash is directed not only against market reform but also—and maybe more so—against discredited, corrupt, ossified, oligarchical party elites. Also, in comparative perspective, Venezuela is one of the Latin American countries where market reform has advanced most haltingly and has always confronted particularly strong opposition. In my view, the election of current president Hugo Chávez reflects less rejection of the new market system than longstanding refusal to enact the market reform program. Since other Latin American countries have overcome this resistance, the resurgence of anti-neoliberal populism in Venezuela does not foreshadow the future of Latin America. Instead, it is a remnant of the past.

Also, President Chávez has not yet defined the economic orientation of his government; he has actually maintained contact with some of the neoliberal experts who had collaborated with market reformer Carlos Andrés Pérez (whom Chávez tried to overthrow in the coup attempt of February 1992). I would not be surprised if after firmly consolidating political power, Chávez decided to embrace determined market reform. A similar turnaround occurred in Ghana in the early 1980s: Jerry Rawlings initially spouted radical-populist rhetoric, but when he noticed that radical populism did not improve the economy, he made a drastic turnaround and adopted orthodox adjustment. Maybe Chávez will act in a similar way and turn into the protagonist of belated market reform in Venezuela.

In general, I see Latin America's new democracies as more resilient and more compatible with neoliberalism than Professor Graham considers it to be. These new democracies have survived severe economic and political crises as well as brutal adjustment measures that according to most observers in the 1980s would undermine democracy. Also, in most cases, market reforms have elicited much less popular rejection and protest than most scholars expected, making the recourse to authoritarian imposition "unnecessary." In fact, contemporary Latin America has seen the emergence of a sizable new force, namely, comprehensive, consistent liberalism. As Professor Graham shows in his interesting historical analysis, economic and political liberalism traditionally diverged in the region. Economic liberalism used to be an elite project associated with authoritarian, antiliberal politics; and political liberals were always critical of economic liberalism. But in recent years, economic and political liberalism have converged. For the first time, there are significant party forces that are both economically and politically liberal, for example, the Chilean Concertación and the liberal wing of Renovación Nacional; the Partido da Social Democracia Brasileira and sectors of the Partido da Frente Liberal in Brazil; parts of the Partido Revolucionario Institucional and Partido de Acción Nacional in Mexico and of the Argentine Unión Cívica Radical. The emergence of this unprecedented combination of economic and political liberalism favors both the survival of democracy and the sustainability of market reform.

In sum, I am more optimistic about the future than Professor Graham. His paper correctly stresses the repeated cycles of democratic transition

and democratic breakdown, of the adoption and rejection of the market
model in Latin American history. But during the last three decades, this
historical dynamic has—in my view—changed somewhat, due to the striking failures of the last round of authoritarian regimes and the tremendous
problems of the decaying statist, protectionist economic systems.
Specifically, there has been a revaluation of liberal democracy and of liberal economics that is unlikely to erode quickly. This value change holds
promising prospects for the foreseeable future.

References

Kahler, Miles. 1990. "Orthodoxy and Its Alternatives: Explaining Approaches to
    Stabilization and Adjustment." In *Economic Crisis and Policy Choice*, edited by Joan
    M. Nelson. Princeton, NJ: Princeton University Press.

The Politics of
Administrative Reform:
Intractable Dilemmas and
Improbable Solutions

The Politics of Administrative Reform: Intractable Dilemmas and Improbable Solutions

BEN ROSS SCHNEIDER
Northwestern University

Introduction: New Institutional Economics and the Political Dilemmas of Reform[1]

By the late 1980s, after a decade or so of "first-generation reforms" that involved extensive dismantling of state interventions in the economy, building administrative capacity rose to the top of the reform agenda in developing countries and among the multilateral development banks.[2] The 1997 World Development Report, *The State in a Changing World*, was perhaps the most widely publicized indication of this shift, but other publications from governments and multilateral development banks repeated the conclusion that delivering social services, getting resources to the very poor, improving the environment for business by reducing corruption and revamping the judiciary, and regulating newly freed markets all required high-quality public administration. Advocates differed sometimes on the types of reform they favored (these types of reforms will be discussed more below), but these differences detracted little from the consensus on the necessity of administrative reform. While a consensus formed on the desirability of administrative reform, which typically includes diverse policies designed to make public bureaucracies more efficient, accountable, and honest, analysis about how to get it lagged. What was often missing (quite clearly in the case of the 1997 World Development Report) was an appreciation and assessment of the politics of administrative reform—politics that are not at all simple or easy.

In an ideal model of successful reform, the political process in democratic systems can be divided into three stages. In the first stage, parties, leaders in civil society, and politicians overcome obstacles to collective action to elect proreform candidates. Second, the newly elected proreform legislators cooperate with the reformist president to enact reform policies. Third, once enacted, the president (the principal) then delegates implementation to his or her subordinates (agents) in the executive bureaucracy.[3] Compared with many other kinds of economic and political reforms, administrative reform encounters especially severe problems at all three stages of this stylized model: election, enactment, and implementation.

On the input or electoral side, the politics of administrative reform are characterized by an intractable dilemma of collective action. The potential beneficiaries of administrative reform are dispersed and disorganized, and each individual beneficiary would gain almost nothing if reform proposals were to succeed. Even if elected on a proreform platform, individual politicians have incentives, once in office, to use the bureaucracy to further their own individual political careers at the expense of general reform initiatives. In other words, elected politicians face a second-stage collective action problem of their own. In clientelist political systems, for example, individual politicians will have incentives to keep their own administrative sources of patronage off the reform agenda (see especially Geddes 1994). Moreover, the opponents of reform (such as unions of public employees) are concentrated; they often perceive their potential losses as enormous and generally have close contact with legislators. In the short run these opponents can raise the political costs to legislative reformers. For these deductive reasons, there are few grounds to hope that reform proposals will emerge from electoral campaigns or elected legislatures.

On the output or implementation side, even if reforms somehow get enacted, they are likely to run into severe principal-agent problems at the third stage of implementation. Ministers and top appointees (the president's direct agents) have their own policy agendas and have little interest in trying to fix the car they are driving (Heredia and Schneider forthcoming). Each top appointee is expected to get on with his or her government function—health care, education, or financial regulation, for example— and cannot afford to divert scarce time and resources to a long-term program of administrative reform with uncertain payoffs. Below this top level is a vast hierarchical pyramid of thousands and thousands of agents, and agents of agents. Most of the economic restructuring in the first-generation of neoliberal reforms involved only a few agents, who privatized state firms, removed trade barriers and government regulations, and stabilized the economy. Dismantling the developmental state can be done without much manpower. In programs of administrative reform, in contrast, the agents number in the tens or hundreds of thousands. Moreover, these agents are precisely the bureaucrats who were diagnosed as the problem in the frontal attack on the state in first-generation reforms, and they are not therefore likely to embrace a plan they perceive as hostile to them. If top and middle-level bureaucrats choose to thwart the implementation of administrative reform, they have the advantage of an enormous information assymetry and can stymie their hierarchical superiors by withholding or distorting information.

In terms of theory drawn from the new institutional economics, especially the parts dealing with collective action, principals, and agents, administrative reform seems next to impossible, even compared with other difficult reforms; it therefore requires a special political alchemy or sleight of hand. Empirically, the list of failed proposals for administrative reform from the twentieth century is of course almost endless and provides a good deal of prima facie confirmation for the theoretical pessimism. Yet, reforms do occasionally get enacted and implemented, at least partially, and from a policy perspective this subset of successful cases merits special attention. Theories of principals, agents, and collective action are best at identifying the obstacles; it is necessary to venture further, theoretically and empirically, to analyze how some reformers have overcome, or more often circumvented, these obstacles.

So how, empirically, have reformers in developing countries managed to get anything done at all? The major thrust of the arguments detailed below is that administrative reform has a better chance of being enacted if reformers bring in unwilling, unintended, or in some cases unwitting allies. A first component of this strategy is to attach administrative reform, like a parasite, to other more politically favored kinds of overarching reforms such as macroeconomic stabilization or democratizing political reforms. These "hosts" can advance administrative reform further than it can go on its own. In addition, reformers can seek out "peripheral" allies. These allies are often from outlying and poorer regions of the country. They stand to lose little from administrative reform and can be compensated for a log roll vote for reform (that is, trading their support for reform in exchange for votes on another issue). Lastly, although captive allies such as the unions in a governing labor party are not likely to be mobilizable allies, the restraint of being allied to the reforming government nevertheless reduces potential opposition.

Three Types of Reform: Weberian, Accountability, and Managerial

Before turning to an analysis of the political alchemy of reform, some conceptual clarifications are in order. First, the focus of this discussion is restricted to master plans for reform of much or most of the executive branch of the central government. A lot of meaningful and lasting reform takes place more incrementally, in particular departments, or at the local level; however, these reforms encounter different kinds of political obstacles and solutions.[4] Segmented reforms of administration in, say, health clinics, primary education, or central banking have particular political dynamics due to the nature of the "bureaucrats" and their organizations (teachers' unions or doctors' associations) and mobilizable proreform allies.[5]

Furthermore, most reform programs, or major components of them, can be classified analytically as either Weberian, accountability, or managerial reforms (see Table 1 and Heredia and Schneider forthcoming for a fuller discussion of this typology). Each type of reform attempts to fix a different problem in the bureaucracy and each gives priority to a separate set of administrative and institutional measures. Weberian reforms, also called civil service reforms, are intended to reduce clientelism, corruption,

---

TABLE 1: **Three Models of Administrative Reform**

	Weberian	**Managerial**	**Accountability**
Diagnosis	Personalism, clientelism, patrimonialism, particularism	Inefficiency, red tape, inflexibility	Abuse of power, arbitrariness, lack of accountability, unresponsiveness (to citizens)
Goals	Universalism, professionalism, meritocracy, honesty	Efficiency, responsiveness (to clients), flexibility	Democratic control (directly by citizens, or indirectly by legislatures)
Administrative Measures	Entrance exams, tenure, promotion by merit, oversight, salary increases, rules	Management contracts, competition among agencies, decentralization, end tenure	Legislative oversight, nominee confirmation, citizen participation
Potential Negative Byproducts	Rigidity, loss of accountability, inefficiency	Clientelism, loss of accountability	Politicization, excessive delays, cumbersome procedures

Source: Heredia and Schneider (forthcoming)

and politicization by imposing extensive rules for bureaucratic conduct, enacting merit procedures for recruitment, promotion, and job tenure, and generally insulating the bureaucracy from politics. Accountability reforms reintroduce political control of the bureaucracy, but they do so through institutionalized channels of legislative control over executive behavior, by implementing oversight committees, congressional confirmation of top appointees, and extensive reporting requirements. Managerial reform is the newest and hottest approach in the best practice literature, both among Organization for Economic Cooperation and Development (OECD) countries and in the evolving Washington consensus on develop- ment practice.[6] Managerial reform seeks to undo the inefficiencies and rigidities of bureaucracy by stripping away a lot of the rules, especially concerning personnel, and granting administrators, or public managers, the discretion to manage their departments and holding them accountable for their performance.

In practice, many reform programs attempt to fix all problems—clien- telism, lack of accountability, and inefficiency—simultaneously incorpo- rating measures from each type of reform. Analytic distinctions help iden- tify where these composite attempts will run into problems: loose, arm's length controls in managerial reform, for instance, open up opportunities for clientelism. In addition, corresponding to the theoretical obstacles identified in the previous section, each type of reform will encounter dif- ferent types of problems. For example, Weberian reforms run into a brick wall of collective *inaction* in clientelist systems (Geddes 1994). Accountability reforms, in contrast, should be more popular in electoral politics and pose fewer problems in collective action among legislators as well as encounter fewer principal-agent problems in implementation. Fewer principals are involved and they have stronger interests in imple- mentation (legislators who stand to gain from their media exposure, say, in oversight hearings), and there are fewer agents (top bureaucrats with information on the functioning of their agencies). Of course, the informa- tion assymetry, as well as strategic motives to exploit the assymetry, still exist. The differences among the models are most pronounced in the con- solidation phase, which will be considered later.

Parasitic Reforms

Given the difficulties identified in the theoretical discussion and the weak- ness of proreform coalitions, or rather of latent coalitions, it is not surprising to find in practice that successful reforms often come packaged in other overall programs of economic or political reform. Given its own political liabilities and weaknesses, administrative reform gets carried along like a parasite on a stronger political host. The host can be a comprehensive reform project in economics, in politics, or in both together. Reformers in the government often recognize their own isolation as well as the daunting problems they face in overcoming the obstacles to collective action in the legislature. To circumvent these obstacles, reformers tie administrative measures to other broader proposals that can overcome obstacles to collective action. This strategy is not of course without costs, especially for implementation and consolidation. Few powerful "hosts" survive long enough to carry administrative reform through consolidation (and resolve the longer-term principal-agent dilemmas of implementation). A more probable outcome is for the "host" to pass away, stranding the administrative reform in midstream.

In Thailand, administrative reform was packaged with overall political and constitutional recasting (Unger forthcoming). The Thai bureaucracy has long had Weberian practices (see Evans and Rauch 1997), and the financial bureaucracy had a special reputation for competence and political neutrality (Maxfield 1997). However, by the 1990s other parts of the bureaucracy had gained reputations for corruption and a lack of accountability. When the constituent assembly was formed to write a new, democratic constitution, bureaucratic corruption and autocracy were central targets of the reformers. In this case sweeping administrative reforms, especially accountability reforms, were passed quickly. The implementation, however, has not been rapid and it is too early to tell just how far the reforms will proceed. The point here is that at the stage of enactment, reformers used the constituent assembly to bypass parties and politicians and packaged administrative reforms with other democratizing measures.

In Argentina and Brazil administrative reform was an element in the popular stabilization programs, the Cavallo Plan and the *Real* Plan, respectively. Macroeconomic teams in both instances identified fiscal deficits as a major part of the problem, so their attention naturally turned to the government's wage bill. However, the linking of stabilization programs and administrative reform came differently in Argentina than it did in Brazil.

In Argentina in the early 1990s, downsizing was the core element of administrative reform, and President Carlos Menem delegated very concentrated policy power to a small group of technocrats (Ghio 1998 and Rinne 1999). In Argentina, administrative reformers had a harder and longer time getting issues other than downsizing on the reform agenda.

In Brazil, Collor (1991–92) had accomplished some downsizing—in a very negative, acrimonious, and ultimately damaging way (Rinne 1999). The original *Real* Plan of 1994 thus did not focus much on the wage bill (though economic officials were preoccupied with the fiscal accounts). Later, though, once the minister in charge of administrative reform, Luiz Carlos Bresser Pereira, had managed to get administrative reform on the agenda in early 1995, officials in other economic ministries began to see Bresser's plan as important to the continuing success of the *Real* Plan. In the Brazilian case though, this stronger political support backed a much more ambitious reform agenda for the federal bureaucracy than would be necessary just to sustain the *Real* Plan (see MARE 1995).

In Hungary, as in most postsocialist countries, administrative reform was from the start part of a complete economic and political overhaul (Nunberg forthcoming). There were so many simultaneous reform agendas that sometimes ran at cross purposes—taking advantage of bureaucratic expertise to manage economic policy versus lustration (weeding out Communist cadres), for example—that packaging did not necessarily have the same parasitic advantage it had in other countries. What did ultimately give administrative reform more coherence and political buoyancy was tying it to the longer-term, politically popular goal of becoming a member of the European Union (EU). Of all the political hosts, the goal of accession to the EU may be the best for longer term programs of administrative reform. As considered further below, other political hosts can run out of steam before administrative reforms are consolidated, depriving administrative measures of support when they may need it most. Getting into the EU requires a more sustained program of reform as well as maintenance of the reforms once admitted.

The parasitic hypothesis also finds some confirmation in countries that lack both administrative reform and other major reform programs that could serve as hosts. In countries like Korea, for instance, there were no sweeping proposals to reform the bureaucracy and no overall packages to reform the economy or polity, at least until the financial crisis hit Asia in 1997. Reform proposals in Korea in the mid-1990s in the Kim Young Sam government focused on accountability measures that did tie in tangentially with the overall transition to democracy (see Kim 1998). And, there were some signs in 1999 that the government of Kim Dae Jung may be linking administrative reform to the overall efforts of his government to reform development strategy, private corporate governance, and practices in Korean politics. Overall, though, administrative reform advanced little in Korea in the 1990s.

Democratization in the early 1990s was also the context of initial plans for administrative reform in Chile. In addition, the new democratic governments were committed to expanded social programs to redress inequalities generated in Chile's transition, under military rule, to a market-oriented economy. Chile's relative abundance of resources, as well as the new government's modest aims for administrative reform, obviated the need for packaging administrative reform. In fact, much of the administrative reform in Chile in the early 1990s focused on rebuilding morale and expertise in the bureaucracy by greatly expanding spending, in part through sustained real increases in public sector salaries (Garretón and Cáceres 1999; Marcel 1999). The new civilian government could afford these measures because they increased taxes from a rate that was previously very low and because the economy was a growth leader in the developing world until the end of the 1990s. Hence, the lessons from Chile for the majority of developing countries that regularly experience low growth and fiscal crises are few.

The Mexican experience of the 1990s shows the limits of the parasite strategy (and hypothesis); it proves to be, at best, necessary but not sufficient. Mexico had a major economic crisis in the wake of the 1994 peso devaluation and experienced ongoing political crises in the rocky successions to the presidency of Ernesto Zedillo in 1994 and to divided government in 1997. However, the government response to the economic crisis was orthodox and did not involve a major neoliberal restructuring since there was little left on that first-generation agenda. In politics, the government negotiated fairly sweeping electoral reforms but never tied administrative reform to them. Overall, discretionary, political control of the bureaucracy is essential to the way the Institutional Revolutionary Party (PRI) functions and dominates Mexican politics; thus presidents are unlikely to push administrative reform even if there are powerful political hosts, unless perhaps they are worried about losing presidential elections and future control of the bureaucracy (see Guerrero and Arrellano forthcoming and Graham 1998).

Despite the short-term advantages, hitching administrative reform to other broader, politically powerful reforms can be costly. First, the broader reform program can force alterations in plans for administrative reform. In Brazil, for example, getting rid of ironclad tenure for civil servants was one element in the Bresser Plan; but, in the context of fiscal emergency and the fallout from the financial crisis in Asia, eliminating tenure became the central issue in the government's efforts to pass the constitutional amendments required to implement Bresser's plan. Another cost of political parasitism, discussed further below, is that support for administrative reform is contingent on the support for its "host" reform program, and that support can dissipate and orphan administrative reform well before changes in the bureaucracy can be consolidated.

Central Reformers, Passive Partners, and Peripheral Allies

Because of the intractable problems of building proreform coalitions through electoral campaigns and party platforms, reform proposals more often emerge from small groups or "change teams" in the executive branch that have special support from the president.[7] The Argentine reforms of the early 1990s were designed by a few people in a specially created body (CECRA, or the Executive Committee for Auditing Administrative Reform) with close ties to a few officials from the World Bank (see Ghio 1998). In Brazil, Bresser Pereira took over a small ministry and staff which generated the comprehensive set of managerial reforms. Both of these "change teams" had strong presidential support. In Mexico, in contrast, two change teams, one in the finance ministry and the other in SECODAM—Mexico's agency for administrative development—produced reform proposals, but neither had unequivocal presidential backing (Guerrero and Arrellano forthcoming). The policy implication is that these small, often marginal, groups in the executive branch deserve support. Many of them never gain presidential backing, but those that do need to be prepared.

These change teams also need medium-term support outside the executive branch, particularly if reform requires approval in the legislature. Passage is obviously easier if the President's party has a majority in the legislature; however, majority control is not a necessary requirement for passage, as the Brazilian case shows, though it is probably a prerequisite for the kind of blank-check delegation President Menem got from the Argentine Congress. Nonmajority situations are likely to force some adjustment (sometimes anticipated) in the government's reform proposal. Majority control is also no guarantee that administrative reform will get on the government's agenda.

Geddes (1994) in fact argues just the opposite, that enduring and strong majorities make administrative reform less likely because the ruling party—or rather the politicians in it—will want to exploit the bureaucracy to enhance their clientelist electoral support. In Mexico, inaction by the majority PRI (until 1997) would support her argument. Geddes argues instead that Weberian reforms are more likely when two large parties are more or less evenly matched. Under these circumstances both parties have equal access to patronage, and thus neither suffers relative losses if all parties forego patronage. Among other problems with Geddes's argument is its exclusively empirical focus on recruitment examinations. Moreover, Geddes applies her argument only to democracies that have existed long enough for major parties to alternate in power; she claims that parties gain equal access to patronage resources over the course of these cycles. Few countries that became democratic in the 1980s and 1990s have established regular patterns of alternation, however: Uruguay and Colombia, maybe, but not Argentina, Brazil, Peru, or Chile. Yet, in the absence of party parity, a great deal of experimentation is going on in efforts to reform the bureaucracy. Reformers may not ultimately, as Geddes predicts, be able to root out clientelism completely, but the other significant reform measures they adopt cannot be explained by the party-parity argument.

Institutional *forms* like party parity or party fragmentation without social and political *content* cannot explain much. So, what kinds of coalitions have supported administrative reform? Generally they do not comprise proreform groups but, rather, passive, captive, or peripheral allies. A natural ally of reformers in government would be the outraged middle class. Historically, middle-class voters have supported efforts to clean up government. In terms of a general taxation and bargaining model, citizens in the middle class should be more likely to demand competent services in exchange for the taxes they pay; they will therefore use political resources to pressure for administrative reform. The rich in Latin America often forgo public services and replace them with higher-quality private services (schools, health care, security, and even streets, sewers, and sanitation in many areas of Latin America); the poor in the informal sector do not pay taxes and have low overall expectations from government services. The middle class pays taxes and cannot always opt out of publicly provided services, so their demands would be natural sources of political support for change teams to tap into. There is some evidence of middle-class support for administrative reform in Latin America, but it is most visible in public opinion polls.

There are two obstacles, however, to greater middle-class projection into political debates. The first is a collective-action problem related to the one that Geddes identifies. Citizens in the middle class may have the keenest collective interest in administrative reform, yet they may still vote for clientelist politicians who deliver benefits to them individually (the family may not have access to universal medical care, for instance, but one of the family members gets a patronage job). The second, and related, problem is the lack of middle-class parties. Class-based parties were generally weaker at the end of the twentieth century than they were at the beginning, when parties associated with the middle class pushed administrative reform in the United States and Europe (see Shefter 1994 on the earlier period). Interestingly, in Thailand, where the middle sectors were more politically visible in pushing reform, they did so directly through an independent constitutional convention rather than through the traditional parties (Unger forthcoming).

Instead of relying on a proactive middle-class partner, reformers are more likely to court passive allies. Groups like organized labor may have a general aversion to administrative reform (even if they do not organize government employees), yet if their party is in government they may opt to provide only passive support, or at least they will not oppose administrative reform actively (see Haggard 1997). Peripheral politicians, those from remote and poor areas of the country, may not be "captive" in the way organized labor is, but they are often open to log-rolling exchanges. Especially in electoral systems that overrepresent these constituencies, like those in Brazil and Argentina, these politicians may be relatively "inexpensive" partners in legislative log-rolling (see Gibson, Calvo, and Falleti 1999). Peripheral politicians have fewer—and usually poorer—voters, so that expanding a government program in the constituency costs less than providing pork to a large, wealthy constituency. Moreover, peripheral politicians are more likely to be indifferent to the fate of upper-middle-class bureaucrats who live in the capital and major cities of the country. In Brazil, for example, hundreds of thousands of employees of the federal government live and work in Rio de Janeiro. Deputies and senators from the far north and west are not likely to sympathize much if these bureaucrats oppose reform, especially if federal programs in peripheral regions stand to gain.

Sometimes the support from peripheral politicians is more than just passive. Depending on constitutional provisions and general legislation on administrative reform, local executive politicians, governors and mayors, may also have an interest in reforming national legislation. In Brazil, the 1988 constitution granted all state and local bureaucrats tenure (*estabili-dade*) so that governors elected after 1988 had little leeway in hiring new supporters or redirecting spending: budgets were already committed to the government payroll, a portion of which went to employees hired by previous executives who were often from opposing parties. Governors in Brazil are powerful in the federal legislature, so their support for reform legislation at the federal level contributed to its enactment (Bresser Pereira forthcoming and Melo forthcoming).

Constraining Successors

Much of the literature on reform, administrative or otherwise, focuses on the early honeymoon years in a presidential mandate. Later years and tail-end, lame-duck periods are generally discounted as improbable moments for reform initiatives. Given the presumption that time horizons for politicians are short, little is expected of presidents who are finishing up their terms, especially of those presidents whose popularity ratings are dragging as they head for retirement. Presidential capacity to forge legislative coalitions or galvanize the executive branch is presumed to fade as the term expires. Or, in cases of reelection-seeking presidents, the incentive is to avoid contentious issues. In some cases, however, especially when presidential succession coincides with fundamental transitions to more democratic politics, political leaders may attempt to use administrative reform, particularly Weberian reform, to constrain their successors in power.

Historically, concerns over successors have been strong motives for outgoing leaders to modernize and depoliticize administration. Silberman (1993) identifies variations in the historical patterns of leadership succession in the late nineteenth century across Japan, the United States, England, and France as a primary source of differences in patterns of administrative reform. In particular, leaders who perceived a threat to their continued status, as did English aristocrats during the extension of the electoral franchise in the nineteenth century, sought to reform administration to lock out those they presumed would follow them in power.

The concerns of outgoing autocrats in more recent waves of democratization have not always resulted in reformed bureaucracies, in part because so many dictators leave power abruptly (as in Argentina in 1983). In more gradual transitions with set deadlines, administrative reform is at least possible.[8] One of the clearest examples came from Chile. General Pinochet enacted civil service reforms when it became clear he had to leave power (see Garretón and Cáceres forthcoming). In Mexico, high-level bureaucrats (almost all tied to the PRI) have been debating the merits of granting civil service tenure (see Guerrero and Arrellano forthcoming). Part of the conflict within the bureaucracy and within the PRI revolves around how long the protagonists think they will be in power. Advocates of managerial reforms, especially old-guard PRI politicians like Arsenio Farell in SECODAM, claimed that the bureaucracy at top levels already worked pretty well and conformed to many managerialist precepts. Against the managerialists, proponents of Weberian reforms noted that any opposition victory would destroy the existing, informal managerialism, politicize the bureaucracy, and, of course, leave the current incumbents without jobs. In sum, while succession politics in Latin America have to date generated few deep administrative reforms, the incentives Silberman identifies may yet play a greater role in future transitions.

Consolidation: So Many Agents, So Few Principals

There are special political conditions under which reformers may generate proposals in the executive branch and forge legislative coalitions large enough to pass legislation. Once these proposals are enacted, however, administrative reform encounters new problems because, unlike economic reforms, it takes so long to implement. Over the medium term, favorable political conditions can rapidly dissipate. Unlike first-generation reforms like privatization or trade liberalization, administrative reform does not automatically create strong winners who can then make sure the reforms are not overturned. Administrative reform thus confronts special obstacles to consolidation. While parasitic packaging has great political advantages in the short run as a way of overcoming the intractable collective action problem of administrative reform, the hosts usually die before the administrative reforms are consolidated. Economic reforms either succeed, so that administrative reforms lose urgency, or economic reforms fail and administrative reform is unnecessary. Overall, political reforms generally take longer, but they may also lose urgency.

Unlike many other kinds of reforms or changes in government policy, administrative reform requires the sustained cooperation of the agents themselves. Beyond downsizing, few administrative reforms can survive the long-term opposition of the objects of the reforms. Strategies to overcome this sort of opposition include persuasion, division, and replacement. If it works, persuasion is in principle the least expensive strategy. Minister Bresser, for example, used any and all forums for talking about his reform program in an effort to reach the middle- and upper-level bureaucrats, who he and his team felt would be natural allies (Bresser Pereira forthcoming). They consistently conveyed the message that Bresser's managerial reform would bring these upper levels more autonomy, more resources, and more prestige. Some survey data suggest that the message resonated (Bresser Pereira forthcoming). Reformers can also attempt more Machiavellian tactics. Reformers in Argentina took full advantage of the split in labor representation among public employees; for example, the union for higher-level bureaucrats was brought into policy deliberations, and by some accounts reformers gave it extraordinary benefits, such as advance consultation of the list of names of people to be downsized (see Rinne 1999 for a full analysis).

The most effective longer-term strategy is to hire new bureaucrats and establish brand-new agencies, creating in either case bureaucrats who owe nothing to the past regime and are the primary, direct beneficiaries of the administrative reforms. In addition, through training and self-selection, they are more likely to endorse the reform program even before signing their employment contracts. This strategy is of course not new and was used extensively in the past in Latin America in the accretion of new agencies and state enterprises that formed the developmental state (see Schneider 1999). In the past this side-stepping of the traditional, unreformed bureaucracy was easier because the developmental state was expansive and required new personnel and agencies to undertake the new functions of the state. In contrast, reform of the postdevelopment state takes place in the context of continuing pressures to downsize and limit government employment. The major second-generation goal is in fact to reform many of the traditional, and previously unreformed, parts of the government bureaucracy. Where the strategy of creating new agencies is more likely to work is in regulatory agencies formed in the wake of privatization of public utilities.

The three types of reform—Weberian, accountability, and managerial—have different consolidation dynamics. Weberian reforms confront the most difficult principal-agent dilemmas because they require the active cooperation of the agents who are the objects of reform. For instance, sitting bureaucrats will have to shift their criteria for promotion in order to install merit procedures. Weberian reforms may of course involve a lot of rule making, but compliance is a more difficult matter. Accountability reforms do not rely to such a great extent on bureaucrats themselves, though minimal cooperation is necessary to open up the bureaucracy to outside, mostly legislative, scrutiny. However, the primary source for consolidating accountability reforms will probably come from those doing the accounting: the legislators and members of the judicial branch to whom bureaucrats from the executive are obliged to report. If the accountability reforms shift power in meaningful ways, then legislators should have enough self-regarding incentives to consolidate the reforms. If, however, the accountability measures do not generate visibility for politicians (as a confirmation hearing does, for example) and if, furthermore, the documents and reporting are highly technical, then consolidation by actors outside the bureaucracy may stall.

Managerialist reforms too depend in part on external agents for their consolidation. In design, the increased competition among agencies is meant to provide quasimarket incentives to consolidate the "new public management." That is, if the budget of a school or clinic is dependent on its capacity to attract students or patients, then competition takes care of the problem of implementing managerial reforms. Those who refuse to accept managerialism will lose budgets and ultimately, once the market has exposed them, their jobs. However, this apparently easy route to consolidation is often confounded by financial administrators who refuse to decentralize finance (see Campbell 1995 on the United Kingdom).

Conclusion

To summarize, multilateral development banks, development and administrative experts, and reformers across the developing world agree that administrative reform should be near the top of the agenda for second-generation reforms. Yet, administrative reform confronts numerous obstacles. Foremost among them are dilemmas of collective action and principal-agent relations. Voters and legislators have a hard time acting collectively to promote their collective interest in honest, effective administration. Even if they manage to overcome the obstacles to collective action, the reform measures they enact may founder on opposition from "agents" in the process of implementation. Focusing on a few recent cases of successful administrative reform generated some hypotheses about how reformers could overcome or circumvent problems in collective action and implementation. In particular, attaching administrative reform to stronger political "hosts" and building coalitions with peripheral and passive allies seemed to help reforms progress.

Unfortunately, the fairly narrow comparative analysis in this paper cannot fully dispel the usual pessimism for the future of deep, sweeping administrative reform in developing countries. However, research on the politics of administrative reform is incipient, and trajectories of other bodies of political analysis provide some grounds for optimism. Throughout much of the 1980s and early 1990s the conventional wisdom was that market-oriented economic reform faced daunting opposition from the powerful, organized beneficiaries of the unreformed system. In some analyses governments required great autonomy and heroic reformers in order to enact reforms over the forceful protestations of rentseekers and others expected to lose from the reforms. Subsequent research has increasingly turned up less opposition and much more active support from a wider variety of potential winners, from the beginning of the reform process (see

Bates and Krueger 1993, Haggard 1997, Calvo 1999). Perhaps as research proceeds on administrative reforms, the proreform coalitions will become easier to identify and prove more powerful than previously predicted.

Such research needs to keep a broad focus and examine not only parties and legislatures but also bureaucratic politics and social coalitions. Redemocratization in the 1980s rightly redirected a lot of scholarly attention to the analysis of elections, parties, and legislatures and especially to the formal rules shaping behavior in these new political arenas. Analysis of such rules, both formal and informal, is essential to identifying obstacles to administrative reform; however, analyses that stop there will miss much of the politics of administrative reform and remain theoretically and empirically incomplete. For one thing, much of the initial politics of reform will involve small numbers of reform mongers in the executive branch. Thus, commissions, panels, study groups, and the like still deserve our attention (see Grindle 1999). Moreover, analysis of the formal rules of political contention often neglects the social content: we still need to analyze the roles of labor, rural or peripheral constituencies, and the amorphous middle class.

Notes

1 This paper draws heavily on a larger project, "Building State Capacity in Developing Countries," funded by the Tinker Foundation. For more on that project, see www.nwu.edu/cics/contents.html. I am grateful to Andrés Fontana, Elizabeth McQuerry, and Kurt Weyland for feedback on earlier versions of this article.

2 First-generation reforms are also called neoliberal or market-oriented reforms and include measures like trade liberalization, deregulation, privatization, and generally downsizing the state both in terms of functions and personnel. Second-generation reforms include measures designed to make the newly created markets work (regulatory agencies to maintain competition and judicial reform, for example) as well as efforts to improve the functioning of remaining social welfare programs (see World Bank 1997, 152). Administrative reform is crucial to most second-generation reforms. Administrative reform includes a wide variety of specific measures that alter incentives in the bureaucracy, including merit recruitment and promotion, performance incentives, training, transparency in decision making, and reporting requirements. The distinction between first and second generations is an analytic distinction; in practice first- and second-generation reforms may be simultaneous.

3 Collective action and principal/agent analysis are core elements in the emerging theoretical framework of the New Institutional Economics or NIE. For recent discussions of NIE and its applications to development, see Clague (1997), Burki and Perry (1998), Drobak and Nye (1997), and Williamson (1996).

4   For example, a full history of administrative reform in Brazil would have to consider both efforts to reform the whole bureaucracy (from the creation of the Departamento Administrativo de Serviço Público under Vargas, through laws like DL 200 under military rule in the 1960s, to the Collor and Bresser reforms of the 1990s) and the piecemeal creation of "*bolsões de eficiência*" or especially effective agencies like the national development bank BNDES (Willis 1986, Evans 1995). Overall, see Geddes (1994), Gouvêa (1994), and Schneider (1991). Much narrower political coalitions can sustain outposts of administrative efficacy. For an analysis of reform through pilot projects in Chilean education, see Angell (1996).

5   See Filgueira (forthcoming) and Graham and Naím (1998).

6   On managerialism generally, see Osborne and Gaebler (1993), Osborne and Plastrik (1997). For an indication of managerialism's place in the evolving "Washington consensus," see Burki and Perry (1998: 121–37). For a word of caution in the application of OECD models to developing countries see Nunberg (1995). For an enthusiastic evaluation of New Zealand's experience with managerialism, see Schick (1996).

7   The term "change team" is from Waterbury's (1992) discussion of the small groups of technocrats responsible for implementing first-generation economic reforms. Grindle (1999) analyzes reforms, similar to some kinds of administrative reforms, that devolve or decentralize power away from the reforming president. She too finds that the reforms originate with initially isolated and marginal commissions and working groups.

8   The Brazilian transition of 1985 was gradual and had been scheduled for years. However, the outgoing government did not attempt any major administrative reform, despite preoccupation with possible civilian successors.

References

Angell, Alan. 1996. "The Politics of Education Reform in Chile." Unpublished paper.

Bates, Robert, and Anne Krueger, eds. 1993. *Political and Economic Interactions in Economic Policy Reform.* Oxford: Blackwell.

Bresser Pereira, Luiz Carlos. Forthcoming. "Reflections of a Reform Minister." In Heredia and Schneider forthcoming b.

Burki, Shahid, and Guillermo Perry. 1998. *Beyond the Washington Consensus: Institutions Matter.* Washington, D.C.: World Bank.

Calvo, Ernesto. 1999. "Inter-Sectoral Cleavages, Open Economy Politics, and the Demand for Promotion." Paper presented at the American Political Science Association Annual Meeting, Atlanta, September.

Campbell, Colin. 1995. "Does Reinvention Need Reinvention? Lessons from Truncated Managerialism in Britain." *Governance* 8, no. 4 (October): 479–504.

Clague, Christopher, ed. 1997. *Institutions and Economic Development: Growth and Governance in Less-Developed and Post-Socialist Countries.* Baltimore: Johns Hopkins University Press.

Evans, Peter. 1995. *Embedded Autonomy: States and Industrial Transformation.* Princeton: Princeton University Press.

Evans, Peter, and James Rauch. 1997. "Bureaucracy and Growth: A Cross-National Analysis of the Effects of Weberian State Structures on Economic Growth." Manuscript.

Filgueira, Fernando, and Juliana Martínez. Forthcoming. "Global Paradigms and Domestic Filters: Administrative Reform in Social Policy in Latin America." In Heredia and Schneider forthcoming b.

Garretón, Manuel, and Gonzalo Cáceres. Forthcoming. "From the Disarticulation of the State to the Modernization of Public Management in Chile." In Heredia and Schneider forthcoming b.

Geddes, Barbara. 1994. *Politician's Dilemma: Building State Capacity in Latin America.* Berkeley: University of California Press.

Ghio, José Maria. 1998. "The Politics of Administrative Reform in Argentina." Paper presented at a conference on Administrative Reform at Centro de Investigación y Docencia Económicas (CIDE), June.

Gibson, Edward, Ernesto Calvo, and Tulia Falleti. 1999. "Federalismo redistributivo: Sobrerepresentación territorial y la transferencia de ingresos en el hemisferio occidental." *Política y Gobierno* 6, no. 1: 15–40.

Graham, Carol, and Moisés Naím. 1998. "The Political Economy of Institutional Reform in Latin America." In Nancy Birdsall, Carol Graham, and Richard Sabot, eds., *Beyond Trade-Offs: Market Reform and Equitable Growth in Latin America.* Washington, D.C.: Inter-American Development Bank and the Brookings Institution.

Graham, Lawrence. 1998. "The State in Retreat in the Administrative Field." In Menno Vellinga, ed., *The Changing Role of the State in Latin America.* Boulder: Westview.

Gouvêa, Gilda. 1994. *Burocracia e Elites Burocráticas no Brasil.* São Paulo: Paulicéia.

Grindle, Merilee. 1999. "Audacious Reforms: Institutional Invention and Democracy in Latin America." Kennedy School of Government, Harvard University. Manuscript.

Guerrero, Juan Pablo, and David Arrellano. Forthcoming. "Administrative Reform of the Mexican State: A Managerialist Reform?" In Heredia and Schneider forthcoming b.

Haggard, Stephan. 1997. "Democratic Institutions, Economic Policy, and Development." In Christopher Clague, ed., *Institutions and Economic Development.* Baltimore: Johns Hopkins University Press.

Heredia, Blanca and Ben Ross Schneider. Forthcoming. "The Political Economy of
    Administrative Reform." In Heredia and Schneider forthcoming b.
————, eds. Forthcoming b. *Reinventing Leviathan: The Politics of Administrative
    Reform in Developing Countries.*
Kaufman, Robert. 1999. "Approaches to the Study of State Reform in Latin America and
    Postsocialist Countries." *Comparative Politics* 31, no. 3 (April): 357–76.
Kim, Kwang Wong. 1998. "Administrative Reform in Korea." Paper for conference at the
    Centro de Investigación y Docencia Económicas in Mexico City, June.
Marcel, Mario. 1999. "Effectiveness of the State and Developmental Lessons from the
    Chilean Experience." In Guillermo Perry and Danny Leipziger, eds., *Chile: Recent
    Policy Lessons and Emerging Challenges.* Washington, D.C.: World Bank.
MARE (Ministério da Administração Federal e Reforma do Estado). 1995. "Plano Diretor
    da Reforma do Aparelho do Estado." Brazil.
Maxfield, Sylvia. 1997. *Gatekeepers of Growth: The International Political Economy of
    Central Banking in Developing Countries.* Princeton: Princeton University Press.
Melo, Marcus. Forthcoming. "Issue Areas and Policy Making in Social Security,
    Administration, and Tax Policy in Brazil." In Heredia and Schneider forthcoming b.
Nunberg, Barbara. 1995. "Managing the Civil Service: Reform Lessons from Advanced
    Industrialized Countries." World Bank Discussion Papers 204, Washington, D.C.
Nunberg, Barbara. Forthcoming. "The Politics of Administrative Reform in Post-
    Communist Hungary." In Heredia and Schneider forthcoming b.
Osborne, David, and Ted Gaebler. 1993. *Reinventing Government: How the
    Entrepreneurial Spirit is Transforming the Public Sector.* New York: Plume.
Osborne, David, and Peter Plastrik. 1997. *Banishing Bureaucracy: The Five Strategies
    for Reinventing Government.* New York: Plume.
Ouellette, Roger. 1997. "Réforme de l'État et Fonction Publique en Argentine:
    Changements Réels ou Réformes Formelles?" *Revue française d'administration
    publique,* no. 84 (October–December): 573–84.
Rinne, Jeff. 1999. Draft chapters from dissertation on Brazil and Argentina. Princeton
    University.
Schick, Allen. 1996. *The Spirit of Reform: Managing the New Zealand State Sector in a
    Time of Change.* Report prepared for the States Services Commission and the
    Treasury, Wellington, New Zealand.
Schneider, Ben Ross. 1991. *Politics within the State: Elite Bureaucrats and Industrial
    Policy in Authoritarian Brazil.* Pittsburgh: University of Pittsburgh Press.
————. 1999. "The Desarrollista State in Brazil and Mexico." In Meredith Woo-Cumings,
    ed., *The Developmental State.* Ithaca: Cornell University Press.
Shefter, Martin. 1994. *Political Parties and the State.* Princeton: Princeton University Press.
Silberman, Bernard. 1993. *Cages of Reason: The Rise of the Rational State in France,
    Japan, the United States, and Great Britain.* Chicago: University of Chicago Press.
Unger, Daniel. Forthcoming. "Weberian Civil Service, Accountability, and State Capacity
    in Thailand." In Heredia and Schneider forthcoming b.
Waterbury, John. 1992. "The Heart of the Matter?" In Stephan Haggard and Robert
    Kaufman, eds., *The Politics of Economic Adjustment.* Princeton: Princeton
    University Press.
Williamson, Oliver. 1996. *The Mechanisms of Governance.* New York: Oxford University Press.
Willis, Eliza Jane. 1986. "The State as Banker: The Expansion of the Public Sector in
    Brazil." Ph.D. Dissertation, University of Texas at Austin.
World Bank. 1997. *World Development Report: The State in a Changing World.* New
    York: Oxford University Press.

Comments

ANDRES FONTANA
Government of Argentina

There are some issues regarding the actual and potential links between first- and second-generation reforms that I would like to discuss. I believe they are relevant to the paper's objectives and relate to the difficulties of producing and maintaining political and social coalitions with the political will necessary to support and carry out administrative reform effectively.

The first point refers to the sequencing of first- and second-generation reforms. Professor Schneider argues that the distinction between the two "generations" is a shorthand, for reforms are often simultaneous in practice. However, there has been a chronological sequence in the "consensus" suggested by political commitments, intellectual interest, and international emphasis. The first sequence establishes agreement on the need for structural, market-oriented reforms, and the second sequence stresses the importance of improving the quality of state institutions and, thus, the need for effective administrative reforms.

This sequence may lead to misunderstandings, particularly if the consensus supporting it is interrupted at the outset of a second set of reforms. This interruption could occur as an indication of the end of the process of structural reforms, at which time it is assumed that reforms have concluded or have moved to the margin of the relevant political agenda. The emphasis on the need for a second generation of institutional or administrative reforms indicates that the first-generation reforms were not sufficient rather than that they are concluded or were satisfactorily achieved. In this regard, "first" and "second" are not a sequence but together are a unitary and continuous process.

The impetus for structural reforms is usually signaled by a profound crisis in fiscal policy, governance, or external accounts and may offer favorable opportunities for administrative reform, as the paper illustrates. The paper also shows the limitations and random character of that potential link between first- and second-generation reforms. Perhaps a more lasting effect of the crises that precede reform is growing consensus about the need for fiscal discipline and limited public expenditure. The latter should be seen as one of the major allies of, and incentives for, successful administrative reform.

Furthermore, the intimate relationship between both generations of reforms is worth emphasizing from the standpoint of the credibility and international reputation of our countries. Unlike in the past, the primary role of administrative reform is not efficiency but credibility. The challenge for countries like Argentina or Brazil is not only to become more efficient and competitive or to have a more rational and transparent public administration. As "emerging markets," we depend on a continuous flow of international capital to finance our growth. Thus, credibility becomes a crucial factor.

First-generation reforms have succeeded in increasing stability and business opportunities but have had much less success in increasing long-term credibility—and lowering country risk—for our nations. In this regard, institutions are crucial, not only because of their impact on economic performance but also—and perhaps mainly—because of their significance for the country's long-term credibility. Therefore, administrative reform today constitutes a substantial aspect of any strategy aimed at increasing credibility.

Political commitment to second-generation reforms and the social coalitions that support their viability are crucial indicators of the will and determination to maintain and deepen the achievements of first-generation reforms. This does not question or minimize the importance of institutions for economic growth. But in countries like Argentina or Brazil, reestablishing credibility is an unavoidable priority, and administrative reform is today a substantial component of any strategy aimed in that direction.

The awareness of political leaders, public opinion, scholars, and business figures may be a major source of the political support and determination required for the successful implementation of administrative reform. The most important factor for the viability of second-generation reforms is to show that they are essential to reduce uncertainty and to increase the reputation of countries that depend largely on international capital flows to finance their growth.

Second-generation reforms are today the strongest signal of the political commitment to maintain a moderate level of fiscal deficit and external debt over the mid- and longer term. This seems to be the only path to reduce major sources of uncertainty to reasonable levels within a reasonable time span. After all, our challenge is to leave the club of "emerging markets" and become regular, normal economies.

A final comment regards the crucial role of Congress and the judiciary. Although Professor Schneider's argument in favor of paying attention to diverse social actors and potential coalitions to unravel the dilemmas of political support for administrative reform is convincing, the role of Congress and the judiciary still seems to be crucial.

The local context in which political determination and social consensus takes place is a central concern of the paper and, accurately, is dealt with as a set of dilemmas. Second-generation reforms require, but are unlikely to convoke, the necessary political determination and social consensus for their success. Thus the paper brings up the "host-parasite" metaphor, which seems to be better applied to cases in which political support for the "host" program of reforms derives from a profound, preceding crisis.

However, reforms are long-term processes and require sustained efforts to materialize. It seems very unlikely that the objectives of administrative reform efforts would materialize unless the basic institutions of a democratic political system are effective, transparent, and committed to improving the quality of public administration and public services. This is limited as an approach, as the paper argues. However, it seems to be an unavoidable precondition and one of the "intractable dilemmas" of administrative reform—but not one without probable solutions.

Confronting Fiscal Imbalances Via Intertemporal Economics, Politics, and Justice: The Case of Colombia

Confronting Fiscal Imbalances Via Intertemporal Economics, Politics, and Justice: The Case of Colombia[1]

JUAN CARLOS ECHEVERRY-GARZÓN AND VERÓNICA NAVAS-OSPINA
Colombian National Planning Department

Motivation

Fiscal adjustment packages are traditionally designed to tackle excessive public expenditure; the reduction of current deficit and explicit debt levels is achieved by using a flow approach to government financing. When a long-term perspective is incorporated into fiscal policy decisions, the result is the pursuit of a dynamic equilibrium that is related to public sector net worth as opposed to explicit debt and deficit targets. The latter approach has fiscal adjustment implications that differ from the former, even with regard to the definition of fiscal imbalance.

A completely new set of problems emerges when implicit liabilities such as subnational government financing, financial sector bailouts, public sector guarantees, or other country-specific liabilities, such as the imputable cost of a peace process, are included in fiscal strategy. The feasibility of the entire fiscal strategy depends on congressional and high court approval of reforms which, in turn, depends on the political desirability and constitutional coherence of said reforms. Additionally, objectives specific to each public body are pursued, and thus the public sector budget and fiscal adjustment program are directly affected by the specific needs of different areas of government. This paper discusses the current Colombian fiscal adjustment model and how economic, political, and judicial considerations affect public policy making.

The hypothesis is that the feasibility of a particular fiscal package depends on not only a sound intertemporal (that is, stock) economic approach but also the incorporation of a new approach to political and judicial decision making. Whereas the intertemporal approach seeks to define how the effects and the assignment of those effects are distributed over time, this new approach requires that politics, and the concept and enforcement of social justice, have an explicit intertemporal dimension as well. A static view of politics and social justice may result in an unsustainable fiscal program and aggravate the fiscal imbalances that it is designed to eliminate.

If an intertemporal, cross-government approach is to be implemented, open dialogue is necessary between the executive, legislative, and judicial arms of government so that consistency of their respective objectives can be achieved in time. Recent developments in Brazil and Colombia illustrate the importance of such dialogue.

The growing consensus with regard to taking a stock approach to public financing is discussed in the following section. A third section deals with the flow and stock perspective relative to Colombian public finances and briefly discusses current fiscal adjustments. The final section explores both the political and judicial considerations that affect fiscal strategy and the risk of adopting a static approach to public policy making. Finally, the need for an explicit intertemporal approach to decision making, in all arms of public power, is justified as a necessary condition for the achievement of fiscal and economic stability.

Fiscal Policy

Pursuing fiscal stability via deficit reduction may be conceptually inconsistent as a deficit, in itself, is an arbitrary accounting construction that is subject to changes in accounting practices; it therefore depends on the categorization of receipts and payments. Thus, data manipulation is made possible, allowing misleading balances to be created that invalidate current fiscal objectives. Kotlikoff points out that "from a neo-classical perspective the deficit is an arbitrary construct with no necessary relationship to the fundamental stance of fiscal policy (1993)." The real effects of fiscal policy are independent from the size of the public surplus or deficit and depend only on the extent to which surplus and deficit alter economic incentives through the redistribution of income and expenditure.

Fiscal adjustment in the form of flow correction, as related to the reduction of public deficit or debt, may not represent an effective solution. It may also be misleading to use conventional accounting to calculate the extent and impact of an adjustment package in which variations in explicit government liability (that is, debt) are considered while variations in government assets, or implicit liabilities, are ignored.

Anticipated government responsibilities, which are not specified as legal obligations, can be direct (predictable and therefore expected) or contingent (triggered by a discrete event and therefore uncertain). A government commitment to accept these unknown obligations that depend on future events amounts to a hidden subsidy. This could cause immediate distortions in the markets and, therefore, result in an unexpected major drain on government resources in the future. The relevance of implicit liabilities such as natural disasters or legally binding court decisions is related to expectations of government intervention, which can be interpreted as being a moral hazard, the scope of which depends on the magnitude of government-led efforts to minimize market failures.

Bearing this in mind, a more appropriate deficit calculation would reflect variations in the net present value (NPV) of public sector assets, minus all liabilities. This approach to deficit assessment would emphasize changes to the government's net worth, and constitutes a *stock* perspective of fiscal imbalances—one that allows for an intertemporally optimal fiscal policy path in which objectives are considered in terms of government net worth.

The development of fiscal policy along these lines requires the explicit incorporation of an intertemporal framework that reduces fiscal adjustment to the fall in the government discount rate. This in turn is linked to generational accounting, a system of long-term fiscal analysis and planning aimed at the sustainability of fiscal policy and the measurement of current and future fiscal burdens.

Such intertemporal analysis of fiscal policy is conducted using the fiscal balance rule (FBR), which measures the impact of current policies on the tax burden of future generations relative to that of current generations. Thus, the intergenerational balance guards future generations from having to suffer a higher tax burden compared with that of current generations.

The FBR implies that governments should extract enough from each successive generation so that if it were in a steady state—in which government net worth and consumption grow at the same rate—it would remain there, with no need to impose a larger or smaller tax burden on subsequent generations. It is evident, therefore, that the FBR is based on the efficient extraction of resources from, and allocation to, different generations, as is consistent with an optimal path of government expenditure. An element of long-term analysis is incorporated into the FBR, which guarantees government financing through a dynamically consistent scheme that also seeks to provide equal funding for different generations (Kotlikoff 1993; Auerbach, Kotlikoff, and Leibfritz 1999).

Fiscal policy complies with governmental intertemporal budget constraints, which are, in turn, dependent on the lifetime net payments of individuals. This concept is related to positive and negative flows between government and individuals in terms of taxes, loans, and transfers. Thus, generational accounting is based on the government's intertemporal constraint, which determines the sustainability of the policy. This constraint requires that the future net tax payments of current and succeeding generations be sufficient, at today's values, to cover the present value of future government consumption as well as the government's initial net indebtedness. Thus, the zero-sum nature of intergenerational fiscal policy is revealed.

The achievement of fiscal adjustments through reductions in the discount rate—a strategy that results in an increase in the current young generation's lifetime net payment—constitutes a real adjustment with respective implications for saving, investment, and capital accumulation. Such a policy, which can be interpreted as an intergenerational transfer, can work with a balanced budget, a deficit, or a surplus.

However, when adjustments are limited to flow variables, targets such as deficit reduction can be achieved by manipulation of accounting categories, a reduction in asset accumulation, or an increase in hidden liabilities. These adjustment packages were criticized by Easterly (1998), who defined them as mere illusion. The use of fiscal deception can reduce a cash deficit, but it is only a transient reduction and is not a permanent shock that shifts government intertemporal net worth. Thus, a deficit target is achieved through policies that turn out to be short-sighted; they do not consider the intertemporal dimension.

Such is the example of a reduction in public investment, which might be dynamically inefficient since it deprives the economy of future revenue that could have more than compensated for the expenditure. A further example is the reduction of operational and maintenance spending, resulting in a reduction of current asset values and requiring future spending on the restoration of assets. This offsets the current value of the reduction in expenditure, thus making it dynamically inefficient.

Another way to meet current deficit targets is to protect current public consumption by shifting expenditure and revenue across time. This is strictly a flow manipulation and does not have any structural impact on a government's net worth over time.

Thus, a government can shift taxes over time or delay financial crises in the banking sector by altering flow temporality, but it is obliged to face the consequences of dynamically inconsistent decisions later. The outcome is persistent and aggravated structural fiscal imbalances as a result of the dynamic nature of fiscal policy.

The reduction of current deficits through time reallocation of revenue and expenditure flows may overlook or elevate fiscal risks. Sound fiscal packages may favor budget programs that do not immediately require cash and which, therefore, temporarily hide the underlying fiscal cost. The dynamic nature of fiscal policy calls for an up-front analysis of risks and the future implications associated with contingent forms of government support, in order to guarantee the dynamic efficiency and consistency of fiscal policy.

Implicit contingent liabilities carry great risks and are relative to the strength of the macroeconomic framework, the vulnerability of the financial sector, the efficacy of regulatory systems, and the availability of information; these factors that affect contingent liabilities are in turn related to transaction costs. The presence of contingent liabilities requires that the cost of uncertainty be incorporated into the decision-making process.

Prudent fiscal policies need to be developed within a long-term framework, and policymakers need to be explicitly aware of the long-term consequences of their decisions. This requires a recognition of the fact that short-term flow stability does not necessarily mean fiscal stability. The elaboration of prudent fiscal policies entails, therefore, the construction of dynamically efficient strategies. This, in turn, requires the development of a single portfolio that contains a stock of (complete and accurate) contingent liabilities, public sector debt, and other public liabilities, and which permits the evolution of a correlation sensitive to macroeconomic and policy scenarios as well as overall risk exposure through time. This approach results in the determination of optimal risk exposure, taking into account the state's ability to manage risk and absorb contingent losses.

These strategies depend on the existence of an appropriate institutional framework in which the behavior of political arms, such as the legislature, judicial boards, or the Supreme and Constitutional Courts, is crucial. The importance of policy consistency in the different areas of government, in order to achieve fiscal balance targets through the conciliation of their respective objectives, is illustrated by situations such as the one currently faced by Brazil.

In the pursuit of fiscal adjustment, the Brazilian Congress recently approved two reforms aimed at achieving a primary fiscal surplus equivalent to 3.25 percent of gross domestic product (GDP). The surplus was a condition of the austerity program negotiated with the International Monetary Fund in order to receive a US$41.5 billion loan. The reforms consisted of an increase in pension contributions paid by high earners in the public sector and a deduction of contributions from the pensions of those who had already retired. The reforms were also in line with the Brazilian government's efforts to achieve equality among the public and private sector pension schemes ("Nuts in Brazil" 1999).

However, the Brazilian Supreme Court recently judged such reforms to be unconstitutional—a judgment that will result in a US$1.2 billion shortfall in next year's public accounts. This move, which will result in further budget cuts, has created additional uncertainty over exchange and interest rates. Uncertainty has also developed regarding political support for the reforms, ultimately engendering a lack of credibility for future reforms. Doubt has been cast on the ability of the Brazilian government to comply with the required fiscal austerity program, thus hindering a speedy economic recovery from a deep recession.

In sum, a trade-off exists between long-term fiscal stability and budget deficit and debt target levels, and between the quality of fiscal adjustments and the speed of deficit reduction. This may lead to fiscal opportunism and, in turn, a bias toward excessive accumulation of contingent financial risks and unsustainable, dynamically inconsistent policies. Additionally, the extent and effectiveness of fiscal reforms employed in the pursuit of fiscal adjustments requires guarantees from both the judicial and political systems. Such guarantees require that the policies incorporate an intertemporal framework that includes the dynamic implications of decisions for the long-term confrontation of fiscal imbalances.

The Flow and Stock Perspective on Colombian Public Finance

The Flow Perspective. Colombia's applied fiscal accounting practice has traditionally based the sustainability concept on deficit dynamics; an unsustainable situation has been explained in terms of growing and persistent deficits. The result has been a fiscal policy analysis based on the achievement of short-term goals, such as reducing the deficit in the current period, as opposed to a long-term dynamic perspective. Given the conceptual and practical deficiencies that arise when using the government deficit as a measure of fiscal balance, policies aimed at reducing the short-term deficit have not resulted in equilibrium. On the contrary, short-sighted fiscal policy decisions have resulted in larger future fiscal burdens.

Traditionally, unsustainable fiscal flow refers to the explosive tendency of explicit public debt when considered as a proportion of GDP. Public debt increases each year on a scale equal to the primary fiscal deficit, in addition to nominal interest payments, excluding the portion financed through seigniorage. When expressed as a proportion of GDP, debt declines in accordance with inflation and economic growth.

$$\Delta\left\{\frac{debt}{GDP}\right\} = \frac{\overset{primary}{\underset{}{deficit}}}{GDP} - \frac{seigniorage}{GDP} + (real\ interext\ rate - GDP\ growth\ rate)\frac{debt}{GDP}$$

Thus, if the primary deficit exceeds seignoriage income, and the real interest rate exceeds the GDP growth rate, the debt/GDP ratio will grow without limit.

The average real interest rate of domestic and foreign public sector debt in Colombia over the past two decades has been approximately 8 percent while the average GDP growth rate has been 3.7 percent. Such a scenario is clearly unsustainable when combined with increasing primary deficits as a proportion of GDP. According to Trujillo (1999), the sustainable level of debt for Colombia is 29 percent of GDP under reasonable assumptions of economic growth and money creation. This level is three points below the current figure and seven points below the level projected for 2002.

One approximation of the analysis of fiscal imbalances in Colombia relies upon measures of deficit and debt, which are in turn based on the long-term performance of income and expenditure flows. Stylized facts reveal an increasing gap between the government's annual tax income and expense flows between 1980 and 1998 (Chart 1). The unsustainable nature of this relationship implies that future expenditure, excluding contingent liabilities, cannot be sustained within the actual government income flow framework.

When limited to a study of flows, an analysis of fiscal instability underestimates the real dimensions of the fiscal problem and hampers the design of a sound fiscal policy. This implies that the forecasted deficit reduction, as a percentage of GDP, does not necessarily result in the achievement of an intertemporally sustainable fiscal scenario.

Therefore the importance of pursuing a stock-based analysis of fiscal policy in Colombia is stressed. This line of investigation includes various factors that have an impact on the long-term sustainability of fiscal policy

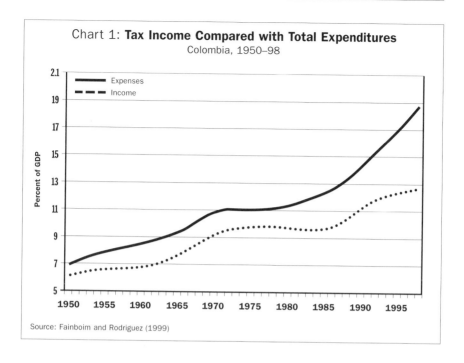

Chart 1: Tax Income Compared with Total Expenditures
Colombia, 1950–98

Source: Fainboim and Rodriguez (1999)

(and which are often overlooked by the simple flow approach). The dynamics of a stock-based analysis require the incorporation of contingencies into the public sector balance sheet, thus redefining the perception of fiscal imbalance through the consideration of major risks to fiscal stability. Furthermore, this type of analysis shows that the underlying, long-term nature of current balanced budgets is unsustainable, resulting from the mislabeling of accounts and underestimations. A stock-based analysis also reveals the importance of intertemporal equilibrium between public sector power arms in the design of public policy—an equilibrium that has an impact on the dynamic structure of a long-term fiscal program.

The Stock Approach. According to Easterly (1999), an analysis of fiscal sustainability requires a study of intertemporal government net worth, rather than of current deficit levels. With this in mind, the Colombian National Planning Department amplified the official public sector balance sheet produced by the National Accounts Office (1997). Implicit and contingent assets and liabilities were included, as well as a reestimation of explicit liabilities and assets, in order to present a more accurate picture of the fiscal imbalance (Echeverry and others 1999). This balance sheet amplification shows the relevant contingent liabilities in the elaboration of fiscal policy by displaying the long-term consequences, and thus the dynamic structure, of the policy.

The following contingent liabilities were included: (1) *Explicit liabilities*: Public body debt guarantees (public enterprises and regional and municipal government); and infrastructure guarantees (linked to traffic volume, income, debt service, excess costs, and delays). (2) *Implicit liabilities*: Bailing out of financial institutions and financial sector deposits; bailing out of regional bodies; natural disasters (earthquakes and floods); contingencies resulting from legal actions against the nation; constitutional obligations with no contractual basis; and anticipated cost of peace negotiations. (3) *Asset recalculation:* Included gas, oil, and coal reserves and the electromagnetic spectrum (that is, air waves such as radio and cellular communications).

The official balance sheet, as a percentage of GDP, is presented in Table 1. The balance sheet, including the recalculation of existing assets and liabilities, in addition to the inclusion of contingent liabilities, appears in Table 2.[2] A breakdown of the estimated contingent liabilities appears below in Table 3.

A grave underestimation of the value of pension liabilities, due to miscalculations, was the most important variation of the amplified balance sheet when compared with the official results. This is a direct, implicit liability that constitutes the most poignant fiscal sustainability problem, due to both its size and its long-term implications. Unfunded pensions constitute a hidden cost of approximately 159 percent of GDP. Social Security beneficiaries (48.5 percent) and teachers (30.1 percent) are the largest parts of this liability.

In terms of infrastructure, contingent liabilities generally consist of guarantees associated with private sector concessions; these guarantees originate when the role of the state transforms from that of a direct service

---

TABLE 1: **Public Sector Balance Sheet, 1997**
(as a percent of 1997 GDP)

Total Assets		**140.5**
	Current Assets	29.5
	Fixed Assets	110.9
	Natural Resources	16.5
Total Liabilities		**78.2**
	Current Liabilities	26.1
	Long-run Liabilities	51.8
	Other Liabilities	0.3
Government Net Worth		**62.3**
Total Liabilities + Government Net Worth		**140.5**

Source: Colombian National General Accounting Agency (Contaduría General de la Nación). Numbers have been rounded.

TABLE 2: Amplified Public Sector Balance Sheet, 1997
(as a percent of 1997 GDP)

Total Assets	**162.3**
Current Assets	29.5
Fixed Assets	132.8
Natural Resources	38.4
Total Liabilities	**251.7**
Current Liabilities	26.1
Long-run Liabilities	225.5
Contingent Liabilities	173.7
Pension Liabilities	159.2
Other Contingent Liabilities	14.5
Other Liabilities	0.3
Government Net Worth	**−89.6**
Total Liabilities + Government Net Worth	**162.3**

Source: Echeverry and others (1999). Numbers have been rounded.

TABLE 3: Principal Public Sector Contingent Liabilities

CONTINGENCIES	BILLIONS OF 1997 PESOS	PERCENT OF GDP
Natural Disasters	**1,360**	**1.1**
Earthquakes	1,343	1.1
Floods	18	0.0
Financial Entities' Bailout	**2,700**	**2.2**
Pension Liabilities	**193,727**	**159.2**
Infrastructure	**7,283**	**6.0**
Roads	122	0.1
Airports	863	0.7
Energy	617	0.5
Telecommunications	281	0.2
Mass Transportation	5,400	4.4
Foreign Debt	**860**	**0.7**
Judicial Decisions	**204**	**0.2**
Territorial Debt	**591**	**0.5**
Peace	**5,000**	**4.1**
Total	**211,725**	**174.0**

Source: Echeverry and others (1999). Numbers have been rounded.

provider to that of a guarantor of minimum sales to private sector service providers. The first generation of contracts included such clauses, whereas recent contracts specify a flexible duration. Private investors obtain a good level of return on their investment, and no public sector guarantee is required.[3] However, the previous contracts generated uncertainty over whether or not public financing would be required in the future, in response to the private sector guarantees.

Contingent liabilities in road construction consist mainly of traffic volume guarantees and, to a lesser extent, excess construction cost guarantees. The former are invoked if anticipated income falls below an agreed minimal level, related to predicted traffic volume. However, if income rises above an allowed maximum it becomes a contingent asset and the excess is returned to the state. The calculated NPV of this contingent liability, to be incorporated in the balance sheet, is 0.1 percent of GDP until 2009.[4]

The construction contract for the second runway at El Dorado International Airport (Bogotá), in addition to requiring maintenance of both runways, includes traffic volume guarantees that are in effect minimum income guarantees; the liquidity for such guarantees has been ensured by the creation of a government fund. Other characteristics of the contract include government compensation for tariff modifications. The NPV of this contingency for the duration of the project (twenty years) is estimated to be 0.7 percent of GDP.

Contracts for energy provision have been granted under onerous conditions; the Colombian government has had to assume the difference between the actual market value and the price agreed with investors. The NPV of this contingency is 0.5 percent of GDP until 2009.

Contingent liabilities in the telecommunications sector are related to minimum income guarantees for the contract holders, linked to the number of minutes of conversation, contained in four-year, joint-venture contracts. The NPV of calculated contingent liabilities in this sector is 0.23 percent of GDP until 2002.

Other contingent liabilities may emerge from the construction of the Bogotá Metro. In this case, the contingency is related to the probability of liabilities being larger than predicted and is partly a consequence of regulatory ambiguities. The Metro Law states that the national government may guarantee up to 70 percent of the debt associated with this project. Thus, if excess costs imputable to the public sector are generated, the national government is obligated for 70 percent of them. These contingencies are particularly important given the risks associated with delays, cost of public services (such as piping), and currency risks related to external financing.

The Colombian case is particularly interesting as well because the government has to consider the cost of the peace negotiations as a contingent liability. The approach chosen was to consider the guerrilla as a business and to calculate the sum needed to "purchase" this business. Hence a calculation of the profitability of guerrilla violence was needed. This was achieved by calculating average expected income and expenditure per guerrilla member; total values were calculated from a figure of 20,000 guerrilla members.[5]

Colombian guerrilla groups present an expected profit of US$430 million per year; the cost of achieving peace is considered to be the amount of investment necessary to eliminate a business with such high levels of profitability. Assuming the guerrilla to be risk-averse, and taking into account a dollar interest rate of 6 percent a year, an investment of approximately US$7 billion dollars is required. However, efficiency gains from army restructuring and the acquisition of superior military hardware should reduce this cost. Not making this investment would be short-sighted, given that the contingent liabilities of a prolonged armed conflict would be much greater. Therefore, attaining peace over the next five years is estimated to have an NPV equivalent to 4.1 percent of GDP.

A dynamic fiscal balance is additionally affected by implicit liabilities resulting from external factors such as natural disasters. Colombia's topography makes it particularly vulnerable to such liabilities, the most common being earthquakes and floods (calculated as having a four- and two-year cycle, respectively). Government obligations after such incidents require the provision of resources for the reconstruction and rehabilitation of affected areas, as well as accommodation for future damage prevention. An estimate of the most recent earthquake in January 1999 indicates that the net current value of earthquake contingency is equal to 1.1 percent of GDP, and 0.04 percent of GDP for flood contingencies.

Another important contingent liability is the bailing out of financial institutions. The analysis of this contingency is based on the current financial crisis and the implications that it has had for the government. Poor performance in the financial sector has resulted in government liquidation of insolvent institutions and the recapitalization of those that have presented net worth deterioration. Recapitalization requires substantial resources and, therefore, additional tax income. The liquidation of financial organizations creates depositor liabilities for the government; these are implicit liabilities that are covered in order to prevent a general crisis of trust in the financial system. The contingent liabilities of the recapitalization process result in a difference between the resources provided by the state and those that cannot be recovered from selling financial institutions in the future. The current financial recession presents contingency liabilities of between 1.24 percent and 1.68 percent of GDP.

Additional implicit contingent liabilities are derived from public sector debt guarantees, which constitute the hidden subsidies previously mentioned. These guarantees avoid tainting central government debt but generate moral hazards, such as the incentive to incur unsupportable levels of debt due to the guarantee of central government assistance should the debt become unserviceable. While these liabilities are subject to subnational government borrowing restrictions, current regulations (based on the 1991 Constitution and laws issued until 1997) are insufficient, allowing rapid growth of regional debt. Since 1997, borrowing has been limited to the payment capacity of the respective regional entity and thus associated with the generation of operational savings. However, the cost of bailing out regional governments is calculated to be 0.48 percent of GDP.

Judicial rulings against the state, which have been increasing over the past decade, are another source of contingent liabilities growing from 0.02 percent of GDP in 1990 to 0.3 percent in 1998. Since 1995 the majority of these rulings have been related to the infrastructure sector, though demands resulting from insufficient provision of social services (health and housing) have also risen dramatically recently.

When analyzing Colombian government net worth, proper calculation of public sector assets, such as oil reserves, is important (see Table 4). Verified oil reserves that belong to the state can be considered as income for the government. Considering that they represent a volume three times greater than current reserves, and taking into account the terms of reference of the association contract with the state oil company (ECOPETROL),

TABLE 4: **Positive Public Sector Contingencies**

Contingencies	Billions of 1997 Pesos	Percent of GDP
Oil Reserves	18,103	14.9
Gas Reserves	11,146	9.2
Coal Reserves	14,785	12.2
Electromagnetic Spectrum	22,657	18.6
TOTAL	66,691	54.8

Source: Echeverry and others (1999)

these reserves have a current value of 14.8 percent of GDP. Equally, coal and gas reserves generate a net present income equal to 12.1 and 9.2 percent, respectively, of GDP. The electromagnetic spectrum is also considered as a source of income, although dependent on licensing; under the current legal framework this resource will provide profits over the next ten years, with a net present value equal to 18.6 percent of GDP.

This revaluation of assets results in a new total value that equals 162.3 percent of GDP, in contrast to the 140.5 percent reflected in the official balance. Government liabilities, on the other hand, increase from 78.2 percent of GDP to 251.7 percent, after the recalculation of pension and contingent liabilities. This translates into a deterioration of government net worth from 62.3 percent to –89.6 percent of GDP (see Table 2). Therefore such net worth should equal the present value of the future flow of fiscal surpluses in order for the transversality condition to be fulfilled.

The amplification of the government balance sheet shows a level of current assets sufficient to cover short-run obligations. Thus, the public sector does not have a medium-term liquidity problem but one of long-term solvency. The implications of this analysis illustrate how misleading the simple flow approach can be in determining fiscal sustainability. In the long-term analysis, insolvency factors are evident, as highlighted by the high value of pension liabilities. The result of these findings is that, in order to achieve a dynamic fiscal balance, the country needs to pursue a greater level of natural resource exploitation, accompanied by both higher economic growth rates and a simultaneous decrease in contingent and known liabilities, including pension liabilities. Of paramount importance are subnational government finance reforms and resolution of the financial sector situation. The results emphasize the importance of using an intertemporal analysis of fiscal policy to achieve a sustainable path of government financing.

Analysis of Colombian Fiscal Reforms. This section presents an analysis of the fiscal adjustment packages implemented by Colombian authorities over the last year. Until the beginning of the nineties, the Colombian macroeconomy was considered stable by Latin American standards. This stability was mainly due to the maintenance of a prudent fiscal stance. Recent instability can be attributed to the decentralization of a number of public sector contracts, among which agreements with labor unions have played a prominent role. Unified budget constraints tend to be disregarded after decentralization.

In this context, the main problems faced by authorities are the size of the necessary adjustment and institutional constraints. The complexity of the situation suggests that the allocation of savings should be made within a three-dimensional space of economic sectors, geographical regions, and time.

The following reforms reflect the main efforts made in the reallocation of savings, along the path described, aimed at confronting the flow and stock fiscal imbalances:

- *Tributary reforms*: These reforms consist of various policies related to tax collection; they have both regional and national implications. The value-added tax (VAT) reform implies an expansion of the tax base, with a simultaneous rate reduction from 16 percent to 15 percent, starting in November 1999.
- *Fuel price liberalization*: The elimination of fuel price controls has created additional income flows for both central and regional government.
- *Modification of the association contract for oil exploration*: The state's participation in the contracts will be reduced from 50 percent to 30 percent after the commercial viability of the well has been established. This gain in competitiveness is designed to result in greater levels of foreign investment and thus in additional income for both central and regional government. A substantial impact on public sector net worth is expected.
- *Reform of subnational government income and expenditure*: The main measures center on a reduction in expenditure. In addition to a reduction of regional pressures on the central government via further decentralization, policies are directed toward more efficient expenditure, including such measures as the rationalization of payroll and acquisition plans and of strategies for funding regional and teacher pension funds. Reductions in central government expenditure refer essentially to public investment, with an emphasis on shifting infrastructure investment to the private sector through a concession system.
- *Reform of regional transfers from the central government*: Currently, transfers from the national government to the regions constitute the budget item with the greatest relative importance, being equivalent to 39 percent of total national expenditure. Additionally, transfers have experienced a high growth rate, increasing from 2.8 percent of GDP in 1990 to 5.3 percent in 1999.

The proposed reform will reduce the pressure that these transfers place on the central government by almost freezing them in real terms once they reach their maximum value as a percentage of national current income. The regional implication of this policy, in terms of decentralized government, is a reallocation of flows, favoring central government finance.

However, specific regional finance reforms have also been presented to Congress to promote fiscal sustainability in subnational governments.

- *Creation of the regional pension fund*: Regional pension liabilities have reached a level equivalent to 39 percent of GDP. This level represents a threat to long-term fiscal stability, and the lack of regional government savings has resulted in serious payment delays. The objective of the policy is, therefore, to direct resources towards the creation of the reserves needed to cover pension liabilities over a maximum of thirty years. The necessary resources will be obtained from the joint participation of regional and central governments. Regional funding is derived from an increasing share of transfers to municipalities.

- *Gambling*: The Colombian Constitution provides for a state gambling monopoly and exploitation of the resource is regulated by one, specific administration. Income derived from gambling is destined for the health sector, which is in an extremely critical situation, adding importance to an evaluation of the administration of the gambling monopoly.

- *Rationalization of the social security system*: One of the most important factors in the current worsening of the fiscal situation is transfers to the social security fund. These transfers represent 30.4 percent of all central government transfers, of which 17 percent are related to severance payments. Not only do these transfers represent a major burden for the central government, but the design of the social security system implies rapid growth of these liabilities. Under the current system, severance payments suffer geometric growth, which resulted in the doubling of this liability between 1996 and 1999. This geometric growth is the consequence of the drawing of severance payments discounted by the nominal value at the moment in which the contribution took place, as opposed to the moment of the last contribution. The government will not have sufficient resources to guarantee this liability if this remains uncorrected.

The elimination of the retroactivity of severance payments has been proposed as a way to achieve long-term fiscal balance from a stock perspective. Additionally, the social security reform contemplates the inclusion of teachers' contributions, exempted until now, and a two-year extension of both the contribution period and the age of eligibility for receiving pensions. These policies should offset what is both a regional and national contingency.

A careful evaluation of whether this fiscal package is sufficient to tackle stock-level fiscal imbalances is beyond the scope of this paper. The purpose is to illustrate how the main problems that were identified in the stock analysis are emphasized in the reforms mentioned, with pension reform being the most urgent.

In the event that these reforms are insufficient to achieve fiscal balance, the result would be a cascade of defaults on public contracts. Default would start with groups with the lowest bargaining power—for instance, pension and wage recipients in remote areas—as has recently been the case.[6] The ineffectiveness of the adjustment could imply further defaults, in which case the last contracts to be affected would most likely be those with international commercial banks and multinational institutions. This could be the reason that Colombian bond spreads do not reflect the current stock problem.

Once the fiscal package has been designed, the government has to confront two independent bodies in seeking approval of the reforms: Congress and the Constitutional Court, both of which can either hinder or promote the government's efforts to impose long-term fiscal adjustments. Therefore, intertemporal budgeting and financing are a necessary, but not sufficient, condition for long-term sustainability. The commitment of these two arms of public power to harmonize their policies with fiscal adjustment strategies, by assimilating the intertemporal consequences of their decisions and taking into consideration the dynamic structure of budget constraints, has become as crucial as the executive strategy itself.

Intertemporal Economics, Politics, and Justice

Economic planning has traditionally been the responsibility of the executive branch of public power and is related to the annual public sector budget. The 1991 Colombian Constitution specifies that each successive new government must produce a national development plan consisting of (1) an analysis of the main problems affecting the country, that is, of the state of the nation at the start of the new government's term of office; and (2) the priorities of the new government for distribution of the investment budget, specifying spending targets for the four-year mandate.

The importance of intertemporal equilibrium in government is evident, especially when considering the extent to which decisions of one public body directly affect the dynamic structure of public policy decisions taken by a different body. The need for dynamic institutional cooperation in Colombia becomes manifest through analysis of the existing relationship between the policy decisions of Congress and the Constitutional Court and the government's intertemporal fiscal adjustment objectives.

What has become evident over recent years is that sound economic planning is a necessary, but not sufficient, condition for the effective planning of public sector expenditure. Indeed, other branches of public power have proven as effective as the executive in affecting obligations, namely, Congress and the Judiciary.

It is crucial to extend an intertemporal approach to public policy decision making to the other branches of public power for at least two reasons: first, in order to give a true meaning to economic planning; and second, to give effective economic content and feasibility to laws passed by Congress and to judicial rulings.

Some laws passed by Congress have increased state obligations, and the remainder of the fiscal reforms are under serious scrutiny. However, the negotiation process necessary to smooth the passage of the government's initiatives through Congress requires that agreements be made with Congressmen regarding investment in their constituencies.[7]

In terms of the Judiciary, the 1991 Constitution created a Constitutional Court to rule on the constitutional status of governmental initiatives, and a procedure was implemented to allow individuals to demand the fulfillment of their "fundamental rights" (known as a *tutela*). Various examples can be cited that illustrate the manner in which Constitutional Court rulings have imposed obligations on the state without contemplating intertemporal budget constraints. This is the result of the judicial purity of these decisions, which fail to consider resource generation and expenditure requirements.

Constitutional Court judgments T-296/98 and T-153/98 illustrate the problems of purely judicial decision making (Sotelo 1999). Following the status change of some civil offenses to criminal offenses punishable by incarceration, the prison population increased. The Constitutional Court subsequently ruled in favor of a prisoner who had asserted that overpopulation in Colombian prisons creates living conditions that violate not only prisoners' dignity but also their basic human rights to life, personal integrity, and health. The court found that Colombian jails were overcrowded, characterized by violence, corruption, and serious public service deficiencies, and lacked rehabilitation facilities. The state, therefore, was not complying with the constitutional obligation to provide prisoners with a reasonable quality of life.

The court ruled that prisoners' rights are guaranteed by the constitution and have "an absolute value, not susceptible of being limited under any circumstance" (Ruling T-296/98) and that the necessary resources for the transformation of prisons be set aside. In doing this, the court arbitrarily decided that this expenditure is more important than social expenditure and therefore must be made at the expense of investment in other areas.

The court ordered the Colombian government to formulate a plan for the construction and refurbishment of penal institutions within three months. Furthermore, the court stated that all work must be completed within four years. This call for improvements in the public infrastructure is outside the judicial mandate and makes the judge a policymaker (that is, an expenditure executor); the judge thus has assumed a role constitutionally assigned to other public bodies. Overcrowding is still at critical levels, and an across-the-board reduction in sentences is currently being contemplated by Congress in an effort to find a solution to the problem.

The difficulties arising from these rulings are not limited to the additional fiscal burden but also include the temporal conditions of the resolutions, which represent an obstacle to the pursuit of an optimal intertemporal fiscal program that will ultimately lead to dynamic fiscal sustainability.

Additionally, decisions by the judiciary affect the fiscal adjustment process directly, as the fiscal package is subject to a determination of its constitutional status. Given that the fiscal package is yet to be approved by the Constitutional Court, fiscal adjustment in Colombia faces a risk similar to that faced by Brazil. In order to increase the saleability of fiscal reforms, marketing devices have to be employed; this paper is intended to be such a device.

Thus, when considering the relationship between the Constitutional Court and government financing, it can be seen that some court decisions ultimately become contingent liabilities on the government balance sheet. Judgments may, therefore, constitute a major risk to fiscal stability and the intertemporal sustainability of fiscal policies. The direct impact of Constitutional Court rulings on the government's net worth illustrates the importance of intertemporal and interdepartmental consistency in public policy elaboration.

However, the autonomous nature of these three areas of government makes it difficult to establish a dialogue that will result in more comprehensive levels of planning for the provision of new public services as well as the maintenance of those already provided by the state. It is therefore evident that sound planning requires a comprehensive strategy, the precondition of which is a reasonable level of communication and cooperation between branches of the government without reducing their autonomy. Intragovernment consistency needs to be guaranteed for the fiscal strategy to be successful.

The rulings of Congress and the Constitutional Court should, at the very least, be compatible with incentives. They should be dedicated to reducing problems and promoting solutions; the implications of the ruling should not be more damaging than those of the problem to be resolved. In summary, Congress and the Constitutional Court should explicitly assume an intertemporal stance when making decisions, considering the effects of their rulings on society as a whole. It should be recognized that a better provision of public services depends strongly on the evolution of the economy and not exclusively on the issuing of laws and rulings that cannot have real economic content when they disregard the state of the economy and the intertemporal budget constraint of the government.

Governability and sound planning depend on Congress and the Constitutional Court adopting an intertemporal approach to decision making. A static approach can only lead to a more erratic path of public expenditure, one full of huge contingencies and an instability of norms. The effect of the existing decision-making structure can be devastating for a country, as is clearly illustrated by the recent experiences of Colombia and Brazil.

The experience of Peru illustrates the risk of a narrow interpretation of the independence of different government bodies and the nature of their rulings. Fujimori deemed it necessary to suspend both Congress and the Supreme Court—a decision that initially received both national and international criticism. The policy was, however, later praised as the only way to bring order to Peru's erratic institutional and economic decision-making process. Commenting on this episode of Peru's history, Barro (1997) concluded that Fujimori did the right thing, as an excess of democracy can be damaging for democracy.

The economic lessons learned over the last twenty years as a result of the exploration of an intertemporal approach must now be learned by the political and judicial systems. No country, in particular no poor country, can afford to be short-sighted when considering its economy and the role of incentives, the burden of contingent liabilities, and the damage resulting from policy decisions that do not promote long-term wealth creation.

Notes

1 The opinions expressed are the responsibility of the authors and do not represent those of the Colombian National Planning Department. This paper has benefited from conversations with Ana María Arjona, Alberto Carrasquilla, Roberto Chang, Juan Manuel Charry, Miguel Gandour, Gabriel Piraquive, Arturo Porzencanski, Natalia Salazar, and Luis Carlos Sotelo. We are especially grateful to Nicholas Perkins for his editorial assistance.

2 For a detailed analysis of the estimation of contingent liabilities and the asset and liability recalculation, see Echeverry and others (1999).

3   Previous contracts involved fixed terms within which a level of profitability was guaranteed by the government. Flexible contract length allows for low profitability to be compensated over time.

4   Balance sheet figures reference values relative to Colombia's GDP in 1997. See Tables 1–4.

5   The average expected income per guerrilla was calculated by considering it as a random variable related to (1) the probability of death of a guerrilla based on the fact that 400 out of 20,000 guerrilla members die each year; and (2) the value of the income variable associated to previously calculated levels of guerrilla income from 1991 to 1994 and their dependence on economic activity. Such data exhibits a high-level guerrilla income of approximately $680 million a year while low-level income fluctuates around $370 million. The principle sources of this income are drug trafficking (41 percent), robbery and extortion (28 percent), and kidnapping (19 percent). Considering that Colombia has been affected by a two-year recession over a six-year economic cycle, a probability of two-thirds was assigned to high-productivity periods. Expected guerrilla income in U.S. dollars = $[Y]$(probability of death) + $[(HY)(P_{HY}) + (LY)(1-P_{HY})]$(*probability of survival*) = 576 million, where Y = income; HY = high-income level; LY = low-income level; P_{HY} = probability of high productivity based upon length of Colombian economic cycles (2/3). Average income per guerrilla member = US$28,800. Estimated guerrilla costs (US$ million): yearly endowment = 6; salary costs = 72; other costs = 72; total costs = 150.

6   Presently some of the subnational governments are in default. Such debt is held by domestic commercial banks, which have bargaining power and are therefore putting pressure on the national government to implement new mechanisms to solve the problem. This situation reveals how this cascade of defaults is reaching a point at which the financial system's stability is threatened, and it is therefore consequential at a macroeconomic level.

7   Prior to the 1991 Constitution, the national annual budget gave members of Congress an endowment to be used for projects beneficial to their constituencies. This practice was deemed a source of corruption and was abolished. Congress subsequently began pressing for allocations from the national annual budget as a whole in order to obtain the necessary resources to effect their own initiatives. Thus, ironically, the abolition of the endowment was self-defeating.

References

Auerbach, Alan, and Laurence Kotlikoff. 1999. "The Methodology of Generational Accounting." In *Generational Accounting around the World,* edited by Alan Auerbach, Laurence Kotlikoff, and Willi Liebfritz. Chicago: University of Chicago Press.

Barro, Robert. 1997. *Getting it Right: Markets and Choices in a Free Society.* Cambridge: MIT Press.

Colombian Constitutional Court. 1998. Rulings T-153/98 and T-296/98. Bogotá: Government of Colombia.

Colombian Contaduría General de la Nación. 1996/1997. *Balance General de la Nación e Información Financiera del Sector Público Colombiano 1996 y 1997.* Bogotá: Government of Colombia.

Colombian Ministry of Finance and Public Credit. 1999. "Reformas estructurales para garantizar la sostenibilidad de las finanzas territoriales y nacionales." Mimeo.

Easterly, William. 1999. "When is Fiscal Adjustment an Illusion?" World Bank Working Paper 2109.

Echeverry, Juan Carlos, Maria Victoria Angulo, Gustavo Hernandez, Israel Fainboim, Cielo Numpaque, Gabriel Piraquive, Carlos Rodriguez, and Natalia Salazar. 1999. "El Balance del Sector Público y la Sostenibilidad Fiscal de Colombia." Archivos de Macroeconomía #115 (June 30), Colombian National Planning Department.

Empresa Colombiana de Petróleos (ECOPETROL). 1999. "La nueva política petrolera de Colombia." Mimeo.

Fainboim, Israel, and Carlos J. Rodriguez. 1999. "Sostenibilidad de la Política Fiscal Colombiana." Mimeo, FEDESARROLLO.

Fehr, Hans, and Laurence Kotlikoff. 1999. "Generational Accounting in General Equilibrium." In *Generational Accounting around the World,* edited by Alan Auerbach, Laurence Kotlikoff, and Willi Liebfritz. Chicago: University of Chicago Press.

Kotlikoff, Laurence. 1993. *Generational Accounting: Knowing Who Pays and When for What We Spend.* Cambridge: MIT Press.

Kotlikoff, Laurence. 1999. "From Deficit Delusion to the Fiscal Balance Rule: Looking from an Economically Meaningful Way to Assess Fiscal Policy." In *Generational Accounting around the World,* edited by Alan Auerbach, Laurence Kotlikoff, and Willi Liebfritz. Chicago: University of Chicago Press.

Polackova, Hana. 1998. "Contingent Government Liabilities: A Hidden Risk for Fiscal Stability." Policy Research Working Paper 1989. Washington, D.C.: The World Bank.

Poterba, James. 1997. "Do Budget Rules Work?" In *Fiscal Policy Lessons from Economic Research,* edited by Alan Auerbach. Cambridge: MIT Press.

Sotelo, Luis Carlos. 1999. "Los derechos constitucionales de prestación y sus implicaciones economico-políticas." Mimeo, National Planning Department (November).

"Nuts in Brazil." 1999. *The Economist.* October 9: 19.

Trujillo, Edgar. 1998. "Cual es la deuda pública sostenible?" Mimeo, Colombian National Planning Department.

Comments

ARTURO C. PORZECANSKI
ING Barings, New York

The very interesting essay by Juan Carlos Echeverry-Garzón and Verónica Navas-Ospina calls for taking a comprehensive, longer-term view of a nation's fiscal affairs and specifically for taking contingent public sector assets and liabilities into consideration rather than focusing, as usual, merely on the balance between year-on-year revenues and expenditures. It calls for a broader understanding of fiscal policy, particularly for the need to rally support in the legislature and the judiciary for whatever measures are necessary to improve public finances over a long period of time. This leads the authors to pursue what might be termed a balance-sheet rather than income-statement approach to public finances—a focus on stocks of assets and liabilities rather than on annual incomes and outlays—in order to help policymakers realize that they cannot ignore certain long-term fiscal issues. For example, cutting a budget deficit via a reduction of investment outlays is a decision that might make sense in the short run but that surely can prove disastrous in the long run. And yet many a budget deficit has been narrowed through such penny-wise, pound-foolish policies.

To illustrate their approach, Echeverry-Garzón and Navas-Ospina then go through a painstaking calculation of the assets and liabilities of the Colombian public sector as of the end of 1997. In so doing, they discover that both have been understated but that, on balance, liabilities are greater than assets. Thus, the net worth of the Colombian government is not a positive sum equivalent to 62 percent of GDP but, rather, a negative sum equivalent to 70 percent of GDP. The authors estimate that while assets are closer to 162 percent of GDP rather than 140 percent of GDP, liabilities are 232 percent of GDP instead of 78 percent of GDP. The biggest difference is accounted for by pension liabilities, which apparently were hugely underestimated in previous government studies.

The authors then review various fiscal reforms now under way, or presented for congressional approval, to deal with a fiscal situation that is unhealthy both in the short term and over a longer time horizon. For example, the taxable base eligible for value-added tax (VAT) is being widened, gasoline prices are being raised, oil association contracts are being modified (to encourage more investment), the revenue-sharing scheme between the central government and the states is being modified, and regional pension plans are being set up. The situation is complicated because the fiscal reforms require the acquiescence of various levels of government and of the judiciary.

This excellent essay could be improved in several ways. First, a bit more background on Colombia's fiscal woes could be helpful for most readers. For example, where and why did the Colombian government go wrong? After all, the public sector in Colombia was known in Latin America for its tradition of conservative fiscal management. The country avoided the hyperinflation of all of its neighbors by preventing the kind of reckless fiscal and monetary expansions that landed the others in hyperinflationary trouble. So why has Colombia been running fiscal deficits in recent years and compromised its long-term fiscal solvency? The deterioration is particularly unfortunate and puzzling considering that the country has nearly doubled its production of oil in recent years and that fiscal revenues have expanded mightily for this reason.

Second, readers could use some additional information on how the assets and liabilities were reestimated to yield such strikingly different results, particularly in terms of liabilities. While the authors illustrate the work carried out by focusing on the eventual cost of the pacification process, this particular contingent liability is dwarfed by the reestimation of pension liabilities, which leads to a shocking result. Pension liabilities are by far the single biggest "black hole" in Colombian public finances, yet precious little information is given by the authors on how they computed the dimensions of this hole. Another item that could use some explanation is the quantification of contingent liabilities related to the banking system. Several banks are now in trouble in Colombia, and they are being helped out by the government. International experience suggests that the cost of these bank depositor bailouts is usually much greater than early estimates, and thus the cost estimated here (the equivalent of about 1.5 percent of GDP) could well be dwarfed by the eventual reality.

Third, readers could benefit from some discussion on the political realities that confront Colombia in its quest for short-term fiscal balance and long-term fiscal solvency. For instance, what are the prospects for domestic pacification, a revised federal-state revenue-sharing compact, or social security reform? What is a realistic timetable for agreement and implementation of needed fiscal policy changes?

Fourth and finally, the authors could usefully expand on the relevance and implications of their stock-versus-flow approach to public finances. For example, if it is true that Colombia's public sector has a negative net worth of 70 percent of GDP rather than a positive net worth of 62 percent of GDP, what should be done about the path and degree of annual fiscal adjustment? Does this discovery mean that the fiscal targets for the next few years ought to be tightened, such that budgetary balance would be achieved more quickly than now contemplated? Should the government aim for fiscal surpluses in the not-too-distant future?

Consider also the unstated implications for the priority and timing of structural reforms. Should privatization opportunities be pursued more aggressively? What about the granting of more government concessions to private investment in infrastructure? And when it comes to dealing with the hefty pension liabilities, does this suggest a more aggressive manpower downsizing policy, or a more aggressive pension reform initiative? Would it be advisable to renegotiate the pension benefits accorded to civil servants?

In sum, the link between the long-term stock approach and the short-term flow approach to public finances needs to be established. Until then, the kind of comprehensive reckoning of fiscal assets and liabilities that Echeverry-Garzón and Navas-Ospina have derived will be of limited practical use—a darned shame considering the terrific research work carried out.

Panel Discussion on Capital Markets and Deficit Finance

Capital Markets and Deficit Finance in Brazil

FÁBIO DE OLIVEIRA BARBOSA
Brazilian Secretariat of the National Treasury

The purpose of this paper is to discuss the role of capital markets in deficit financing with specific reference to the Brazilian case. After this short introduction, the paper is divided into two parts. The first part summarizes fiscal policy in Brazil over the last few years, focusing on the implementation of a vast fiscal agenda despite some short-term setbacks. The second part describes recent developments in budget financing, particularly in strategies for public debt management for both domestic and external capital markets. The final section concludes by providing some perspective on future deficit financing and fiscal policy.

The Fiscal Agenda: Main Challenges and Results

Currently Brazilian fiscal policy is undergoing a dramatic change. In 1999, the primary result targeted was a surplus of 3.1 percent of gross domestic product (GDP). Of this amount, the central government was slated to accrue 2.3 percent of GDP, 0.4 percent should come from state and local governments, and state-owned enterprises should add another 0.4 percent.

The results, presented in Chart 1, confirm the Brazilian government's commitment to achieving the required fiscal targets. The targets have been met for four consecutive quarters beginning in December 1998, and recent numbers indicate that the year-end target will be reached as well.

Figures for the central government, comprising the National Treasury, the Social Security System, and Central Bank operational accounts, showed a primary surplus of 2.66 percent of GDP in the period from

January through October (see Chart 2). Last year, the primary surplus was 0.65 percent of GDP during the same period. The increase, equivalent to 2.1 percent of GDP, was largely achieved through expenditure reduction

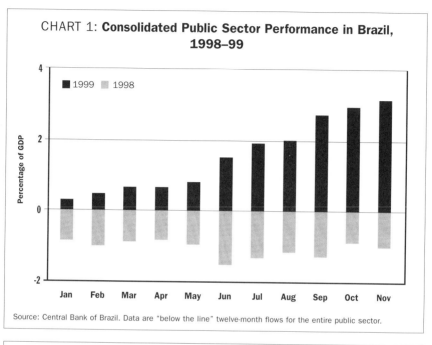

CHART 1: **Consolidated Public Sector Performance in Brazil, 1998–99**

Source: Central Bank of Brazil. Data are "below the line" twelve-month flows for the entire public sector.

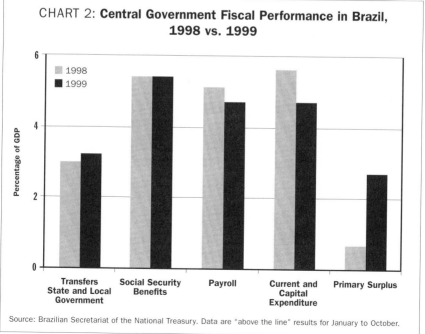

CHART 2: **Central Government Fiscal Performance in Brazil, 1998 vs. 1999**

Source: Brazilian Secretariat of the National Treasury. Data are "above the line" results for January to October.

and enhanced tax revenue collection. It is also important to stress that this result has been achieved despite modest growth in GDP in 1999 and an increase in the social security deficit, which jumped from 0.6 to 0.8 percent of GDP in the same period.

On the expenditure side, despite some rigid rules, budget execution has been strictly in line with targets. Mandatory expenditures, such as transfers to states and local governments and social security benefits, grew by 15.0 and 9.7 percent, respectively, in nominal terms in 1999. Discretionary expenditures, the only remaining area of spending that could be cut, were reduced by 10 percent, demonstrating the major fiscal effort under way.

State-owned enterprises (SOE) moved from a deficit of 0.20 percent of GDP in 1998 to a surplus of 0.64 percent in the first ten months of 1999. The same trend was detected in the result for the state and local governments (SLG), which showed a 0.37 percent surplus through October 1999. This compares very favorably with the deficit of 0.27 percent of GDP during the same period in 1998.

In sum, looking at the short-term flows, it is clear that the government's fiscal stance improved in 1999 compared with the previous year, when the primary balance was not consistent with the macroeconomic framework and the external scenario. However, analysts should not underestimate the efforts that the country has made over the last four or five years with respect to structural reform. In fact, Brazil has implemented a vast and impressive fiscal agenda despite, as mentioned before, precarious short-term fiscal flows.

The first item of this agenda is privatization. Brazil has been implementing one of the largest privatization programs ever. Since 1991, it has rendered US$87 billion in proceeds and debt transfers, an amount that would currently be equivalent to 16 percent of GDP.

Privatization was crucial from the fiscal standpoint due to two of its major effects: the permanent reduction of interest charges as a result of debt redemption, and the elimination of potential equity investments that could be required from the Treasury (as a shareholder) if companies remained in government hands. For instance, in the case of the steel and power sectors, the Treasury's capital support for state-owned enterprises in 1986 and 1987 was equivalent to 2.5 percent of GDP.

Privatization not only has reduced outstanding debt but also has generated some positive "collateral effects" for the country, such as the reinforcement of foreign direct investment flows (FDI). In 1994, FDI in Brazil was US$2.6 billion. In 1998, it was US$26.1 billion, and in 1999, despite the floating of the exchange rate, FDI had reached US$24.8 billion in October and was expected to be around US$27 billion by year-end. According to the Central Bank of Brazil, FDI flows directly related to the privatization program totaled US$22.8 billion over the last four years (see Chart 3).

Privatization has also brought new players to the stock market, which is a very important aspect of the overall process of financing future economic growth. Finally, the Brazilian economy is already benefiting from the efficiency and productivity gains brought by privatization of former SOEs, which were usually overstaffed and inefficient.

The second item on the structural agenda was administrative reform. This program was designed to provide greater flexibility in human resource management, allowing for the required adjustments through the elimination of job stability and the single legal regime for civil servants and through the establishment of more rational criteria to adjust civil service salaries. A major change has already taken place even though additional legislation is required (for example, draft bills on the parameters for public employment and the dismissal of civil servants, and a constitutional amendment setting salary ceilings for the three branches of government). Nevertheless, a reduction of the potential long-term deficit is projected from enhanced control of personnel expenditure—one of the largest budget components.

The third major area was reform of the social security system. The milestone here was the change from a concept of time of service—established

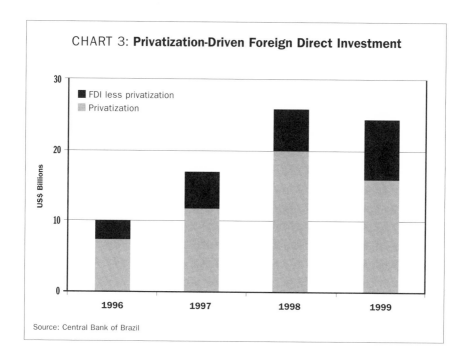

CHART 3: **Privatization-Driven Foreign Direct Investment**

Source: Central Bank of Brazil

some sixty years ago, mirroring the Italian "Carta del Lavoro"—to a concept of time of contribution and minimum age as parameters for retirement. Also, the partial benefit granted for early retirement was removed. Those changes are expected to smooth and reduce the projected deficits for the social security system, until the results reach sustainable levels.

The second stage of social security reform is under way and involves several important aspects. These include reworking the regulatory frameworks between public sector entities and pension funds for public employees, instituting civil servant contributions (including those of retired civil servants) to public pension funds, and, finally, establishing more adequate parameters for private workers' pension funds.

The fourth item on the reform agenda, which is not usually treated as such although it could be said that it has the same relevance in terms of structural change and long-run fiscal effects, is refinancing of state government debt. A major program has been implemented in this area since 1996. So far, the Treasury has signed contracts with twenty-five of the twenty-seven states, and the two remaining states (Tocantins, which is a new state, and Amapá, in the northern part of Brazil) are not crucial to determining the core fiscal result.

The total amount refinanced was around R$120 billion (equivalent to US$70 billion). Under the agreements, the states are committed to generating a primary surplus equivalent to 13 percent of net current revenues, and ceilings have been set for their debt-to-net-revenue ratio. The agreements also limit the states' access to international borrowing from multilateral institutions and through bond issuance.

Several states initiated privatization programs, which included the sale of electricity, gas, water, and sewage companies. Since 1996, states took in US$31.6 billion from privatization (including debt transferred to the new shareholders), out of which São Paulo State's share corresponded to approximately US$13.3 billion.

These contracts included several targets related to state banks, which were closed, transformed into development agencies, or privatized. Five major financial institutions were privatized (BANERJ, CREDIREAL, BEMGE, BANDEPE, and BANEB). BANESPA—one of the largest Brazilian commercial banks and previously owned by the government of the state of São Paulo—is going to be privatized in the first half of 2000. Several other smaller state banks were closed.

This effort has had two effects. First, together with the government's program to strengthen and restructure the financial sector (PROER), privatization of state-owned banks is helping to promote a healthier financial system by eliminating institutions that were usually inefficient and under-capitalized from the economic arena. Second, it closes the important "window of financing" that states have used in the past, when their banks performed the role of "lender of last resort" to finance budget deficits.

A similar phenomenon occurred when some state-owned power companies used their cash flows to finance budgetary expenditures unrelated to their core activities. On some occasions companies would buy energy from federal power generation companies without paying for it, thereby transforming a state deficit into a federally financed deficit. It was a very comfortable and efficient source of funding because it is hard to imagine the federal government shutting off the power to a major city. In addition to causing fiscal problems, this procedure reduced the market value of federal power generation companies. As previously noted, the states' privatization programs are addressing those concerns.

All things considered, one can easily attribute at least part of the swing in state and local government finances of 0.64 percent of GDP to the effectiveness of the fiscal programs monitored by the Treasury. A lot remains to be done, but it is clear that the potential for SLG finances to damage the country's fiscal policy has been minimized.

In sum, the fiscal agenda that has been implemented over the last few years is a very important one, involving major structural changes that address all the relevant components of a sound fiscal policy. It is noteworthy to stress that most of this agenda calls for constitutional amendments, which—after passing the Senate and House of Representatives' Justice and Constitution Committees—require a 60 percent majority in two rounds of voting in each of the two houses to receive final approval. So far, twenty-two constitutional amendments have been approved, most of them in the last six years, clearly demonstrating Brazil's commitment to a new fiscal policy.

It was also true, however, that by the end of 1998 the gradualism in fiscal policy was no longer acceptable, particularly after the failure of the 1997 fiscal package. A tougher fiscal policy needed to be put in place.

This very strong message was conveyed by domestic and international capital markets through the volatility of many variables. Increased spreads for emerging economies, reduced access to new lending, and shortened maturities all affected the overall budget structure and public debt management strategy. These effects are precisely the subject of the next part of this paper.

Budget Financing and Debt Management Strategies in Recent Years

The bulk of the federal budget deficit in Brazil is financed by domestic capital markets, mostly through bonded debt. After 1994, which marked the beginning of the *Real* Plan and the successful process of macroeconomic stabilization, it was clear that the federal government's debt management strategy should be adapted to the new environment.

By that time, public debt structure was almost fully indexed—most of it to inflation indexes, the exchange rate, or to floating short-term interest rates; nominal, fixed-rate instruments represented no more than 6 percent of total outstanding debt. At that point, the basic strategy was to modify the domestic debt structure by gradually increasing the share and average maturity of fixed-rate instruments.

This strategy was implemented cautiously and gradually, since the economy was just starting to consolidate after the stabilization process began and uncertainty prevailed regarding inflation and nominal interest rates. Also, there was very modest activity in forward markets for longer-dated instruments. In early 1995, only two-month fixed-rate instruments were auctioned, and it was two and a half years until the Treasury could sell two-year fixed-rate notes—in September 1997. These were the longest-term notes ever sold in the domestic market. At that point, the share of fixed-rate instruments in total federal domestic debt was about 64 percent, and the duration had increased significantly.

The second auction for the two-year note was scheduled for October 30, 1997. However, in that very week the Asian crisis took place, bringing instability to international capital markets and particularly affecting the emerging market economies. Brazil also faced turbulence in its domestic capital markets, with uncertainties about the sustainability of the *Real* Plan and the virtually fixed exchange rate regime. The Central Bank raised short-term interest rates sharply in order to cope with market pressures against the economic policy framework.

Due to the increased duration of the instruments that had occurred, the cost of public debt was not significantly affected by monetary policy tightening. The Treasury continued to issue fixed-rate securities but, instead of a two-year maturity, the offer structure was gradually shortened because of the market's reluctance to buy longer-dated securities. Maturity was first shortened to one year, then six months, then three months, and finally to two months at the first successful fixed-rate instrument auction after the Asian Crisis in mid-December, 1997. The maturity-lengthening process restarted, and by March 1998 one-year fixed-rate public debt instruments were being auctioned.

The process was interrupted again in mid-1998 in the wake of three sorts of problems. The first was turbulence in international capital markets associated with Russia. Second, 1998 was an election year in Brazil and the opposition party candidate was running ahead of the president, increasing uncertainties about the economic outlook and thus sparking volatility in the domestic capital market. The Central Bank target for overnight rates (the SELIC rate) was also reduced—a move that was not received well by the market. Finally, the spread between Central Bank rates and effective market rates widened, directly affecting the Treasury's ability to sell fixed-rate securities.

In this environment, a new reduction in the maturity profile structure of the offer was required in order to allow the Treasury to keep selling fixed-rate securities. However, it was appropriate for the Treasury to go into a critical position in terms of the "perceived" refinancing risks by further shortening the average maturity. There were already some signs of concern from international and domestic capital markets about public debt profile. So there was a trade-off between duration and the Treasury's refinancing risk, and the decision was to minimize the latter by using floating-rate instruments. The strategy was successful in keeping the average yield at very comfortable levels, but it did so at the cost of a sharp reduction in domestic debt duration.

In 1999, the Treasury continued to issue floating-rate instruments (one- and two-year notes), and by April fixed-rate instruments represented no more than 4 percent of total domestic debt. The Treasury gradually resumed issuing shorter fixed-rate instruments while monitoring the total debt average maturity (then at about ten months) in order to avoid unnecessary noise in this area (see Chart 4 for September figures).

As for external debt, the Treasury's borrowing program is not driven by budget financing demands. Since 1995, when Brazil returned to international capital markets, the Treasury has borrowed about US$18.8 billion in nineteen transactions.[1] Out of this total, around US$5.3 billion were bond exchange transactions and did not involve new money. In net terms, the Treasury borrowed some $13.6 billion in cash over almost five years (averaging about US$2.7 billion per year).

In this context, international borrowing is not really relevant for budget financing, which is mostly done through the domestic capital market. Of course the country faced a very difficult situation in late 1998 and early 1999, and the support package arranged by the international community was extremely important to the economy's recovery and for dealing with

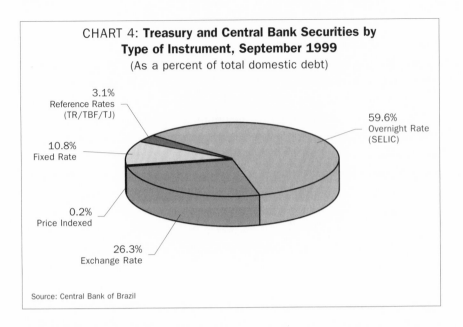

CHART 4: Treasury and Central Bank Securities by Type of Instrument, September 1999
(As a percent of total domestic debt)

3.1% Reference Rates (TR/TBF/TJ)

59.6% Overnight Rate (SELIC)

10.8% Fixed Rate

0.2% Price Indexed

26.3% Exchange Rate

Source: Central Bank of Brazil

the balance-of-payments constraints. However, this was an atypical situation, and the Treasury's strategy towards international capital markets follows a different approach.

In fact, the first objective is to establish benchmarks in strategic markets (dollar, euro, and yen) in order to build and maintain some reference of Brazilian sovereign risk for the relevant segments of the yield curve and to pave the way for other Brazilian borrowers, both public and private. Establishing such benchmarks is important because the domestic capital market in Brazil does not yet provide long-term financing at rates compatible with the expected rate of return on projects.

A second objective is to develop a solid investor base for Brazilian issues in order to attract new investments and to demonstrate the country's profound transformation over the past five years. It could be said that the Treasury's external borrowing program has played a catalyzing role in the success of the privatization process and the massive FDI flows with which it is associated.

The third objective is related to balance-of-payments requirements. Since 1995, two of the nineteen transactions have been denominated in yen, twelve in euro or other European currencies, and five in global bonds. The turbulence involving emerging economies in general, and Brazil in particular, deeply affected country access to international capital markets. The magnitude of change can been seen in the widening spreads for sovereign bonds. In June 1997, the Treasury issued a global, thirty-year bond with a 395 basis point spread; two years later, a global, ten-year bond was bearing an 850 basis point spread.

However, more important than the yield is the access to the market itself, which is central to financing the current account deficit. So, when borrowers faced several "closed doors," with a very low roll-over rate for credit lines and bonds, the Treasury played a key role in providing the appetite for Brazilian risk in several transactions throughout 1999, mainly in the new and promising eurobond market. The goal was accomplished, and domestic borrowers, despite the cost increase, are gradually returning to the international capital markets.

Perspectives for Fiscal Policy, Deficit Financing, and Debt Management Strategy

Brazil's fiscal policy target for 2000 is an overall public sector primary surplus of 3.25 percent of GDP. The federal government budget was sent to Congress with a primary surplus of 2.65 percent of GDP, and, for the first time, this target was established by a legal instrument (the Budget Guidelines Law).

The privatization pipeline is very strong. In October, an important legal obstacle to the privatization of the electrical generation facility, FURNAS, was removed. Two other electrical generation facilities, CHESF and ELETRONORTE, are also scheduled to be sold in 2000. The federal government is concluding negotiations with the state of São Paulo to speed up the sale of its state-owned bank, BANESPA. CESP-Paraná will most likely be divided into two parts and also privatized next year, together with other power distribution companies owned by the states of Paraiba, Pernambuco, Pará, Maranhão, and Paraná.

Regarding debt management, the objective is to increase the share and the maturity of fixed-rate securities. The core of the Treasury's strategy is to lengthen the duration of the debt in order to increase the predictability of debt service, reduce budget risks, improve the effectiveness of monetary policy, and develop the domestic capital market. As of late 1999, this has not been an easy task, given that forward markets are liquid only for the next six months and that the possibility of a one-year note is not there yet. However, as in the past, this process will be carried out very cautiously.

The Treasury has not issued dollar-linked securities since January 1999, and there is no intention to do that in the short run. Although it could be appropriate in a virtually fixed exchange rate regime, it would not fit well in a floating exchange rate regime. The Treasury's goal is to use the predictability of the exchange rate to issue long-term securities (three to five years), extend the average maturity of public debt, and provide a sort of domestic benchmark until fixed-rate instruments can again be established.[2]

The development of the domestic capital market is a major priority for the federal government. To achieve this, one important measure is to reduce the number of auctions. There are now four auctions every week, and it is clear that this heavy schedule reduces investor interest in the events and does not support the development of the secondary market. However, the new debt auction schedule will be implemented very carefully so as to preserve the Treasury's refinancing risk at safe levels.

In the same context, the Treasury is planning to reduce the number of debt instruments offered to the market. Currently, securities can be linked to the reference rate set by the Central Bank (TR), the dollar, price indexes, or a fixed rate. It is likely that this diversity will lead to the pulverization of the secondary market, with negative effects on its liquidity as well as an increase in the issuer's cost of financing in the primary market.

The Treasury and the Central Bank of Brazil intend to publish monthly auction schedules, hopefully three or four months ahead of time, in order to increase predictability, attract more investors, and improve liquidity in some specific segments. The implementation of the "reverse auction" not only will enhance liquidity for longer-dated debt instruments but also will help to adjust the public debt profile to the new environment. Some market incentives to public debt dealers will be established, with more strict performance criteria in order to transform them into effective marketmakers.

Finally, the Treasury is planning the implementation of a "domestic exchange" involving the so-called privatization currencies. When several SEOs were sold or closed down, the Treasury took over their liabilities and refinanced them through privatization currencies. These are long-term bonds (the average maturity today is around fifteen years) bearing below-market interest rates. These could be called the Brazilian domestic Bradys. The problem is that there are seventy-five different bonds on the market, most with very low liquidity, which reduces their potential to operate as benchmarks for long-term transactions.

The plan is to hold an auction in which the Treasury would offer new five-, ten-, and fifteen-year securities in exchange for the privatization currencies, on a strictly voluntary basis. Cash could be accepted, but there has still been no decision regarding floors or ceilings for this portion. However, this will not be the focus of the auction since the idea is to improve the liquidity of these instruments, reduce the number of different instruments traded in the market, and at the same time provide a sort of benchmark. The new security will be indexed to the same price index used with most privatization currencies, which means there will be no increase in the share of indexed domestic debt.

The new bond issue may prove to be an important instrument for funds, insurance companies, and others who would like to hedge long-term indexed liabilities. At the same time, it could help the Treasury to lengthen the average maturity of the outstanding domestic debt.

In sum, the Treasury's debt management strategy is to increase duration, which will be done basically through the increased issuance of fixed-rate securities. At the same time, the federal government (the Treasury and the Central Bank of Brazil) will be working to develop domestic capital markets adequately, focusing on the establishment of an effective yield curve covering all relevant maturities.

Until that goal is accomplished, it is important to keep borrowing from international capital markets as the Treasury did in 1999, with three-, five-, and seven-year euro transactions, as well as with the 2004/2009 global bonds. A new yen transaction was planned for the beginning of 2000, once that market appears to be opening up for emerging market risk.

The Treasury will continue to be present in those markets, but not as a heavy borrower. In fact, the Treasury's external debt amortization profile is comfortable and enjoys the availability of a deep and liquid domestic market that, although requiring further improvements, already provides necessary budget financing.

Notes

1 This amount does not include the external support package made available to the country in the end of 1998.

2 Brazil has a peculiar situation in that there are two issuers of bonded debt at the federal level: the Central Bank and the Treasury. The Treasury is now replacing the Central Bank, which is getting out of this business. In a few years, the Treasury will be the sole issuer. The Central Bank has been issuing dollar-linked securities for exchange rate or monetary policy purposes but not to finance the budget, an action forbidden by the Constitution.

Financing Deficits in Peru

CARLOS BOLOÑA
San Ignacio de Loyola University, Peru

Iwould like to thank the Federal Reserve Bank of Atlanta for this invitation. It's my pleasure to be here and share some experiences about deficit finance in capital markets, wherever they may apply. My experience is the case of Peru.

In the 1980s in Peru, the populist model was applied during the first half of the decade by President Fernando Belaunde and by Alan Garcia during the second five-year period. It was a pure populist model that came hand-in-hand with democracy. Democracy has been connected with a populist model since the 1970s, when we had a socialist military regime that failed completely. Belaunde gave us a fiscal deficit of about 7.1 percent of gross domestic product (GDP), an average yearly inflation of 108 percent, and a growth rate of zero during his administration. He also defaulted on our debt after the Mexican crisis in 1982.

Garcia went further with the populist model. He decided not to pay the country's debts, or to pay only 10 percent of exports, which meant defaulting on all the banks, defaulting on all the Paris Club members, and defaulting on international financial institutions like the World Bank, the Inter-American Development Bank (IDB), and the International Monetary Fund (IMF). Thus, thanks to Garcia, we became members of the Pariah Club. Along with Libya, Haiti, Liberia, and North Korea, we were members of the group of ineligible countries that did not receive a single cent from the world economy. Therefore, getting access to capital markets in order to finance our deficit was hard, to say the least.

Yet Garcia managed to get some international capital. Then he decided that he was going to apply a heterodox approach to the economy in which it didn't matter how large the deficit became. What was important was to give the people what they wanted. Not surprisingly, the fiscal deficit and the quasifiscal deficit reached 16 percent of GDP. The GDP per capita reached US$720, an amount lower than that of 1960. One can't really look at the gross numbers, which don't mean anything after hyperinflation. Garcia's legacy was 2.2 million percent inflation in five years, minus 7 percent GDP growth, and a loss of US$300 million in net reserves. This meant isolation in every way. They didn't even accept our collect calls. "Peru? Sorry, we don't accept collect calls from Peru."

So, that was Alan Garcia's legacy. We definitely had an inflation tax. Since taxation in Peru was reduced to 4 percent of GDP, the inflation tax was very easily around 10 percent or more of GDP. Inflation reached almost 8,000 percent in 1990, 60 percent a month, and 2 percent a day. We started to look at inflation on a daily basis. A long-term bank loan was five days, medium-term was two days, and short-term was measured in hours. Moreover, the interest rate was 60 percent a month (see Chart 1).

As you can imagine, this was a lot to deal with. When Alberto Fujimori ran for elections, he won by saying what he was not going to do. He said, "I am not going to produce a shock, I am not going to privatize, and I am not going to fire public employees." His program was very simple: *Trabajo, tecnología, y honestidad.* Work, technology, and honesty—that was his program. And that's the best way to win elections: Not saying

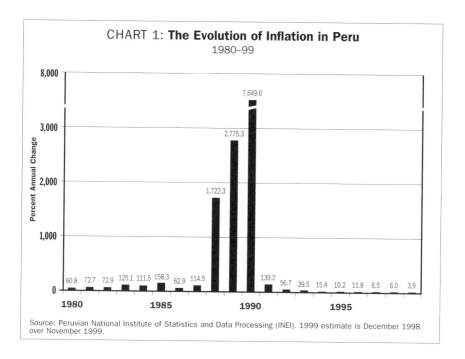

CHART 1: **The Evolution of Inflation in Peru**
1980–99

Source: Peruvian National Institute of Statistics and Data Processing (INEI). 1999 estimate is December 1998 over November 1999.

anything and doing things afterward. Carlos Menem in Argentina and our good friend Fujimori did it the same way.

How I ended up working with Fujimori is a long story. I didn't vote for him, I didn't believe he was right for Peru, and I thought he was going to be more of the same as Garcia. But circumstances led me to discuss his economic program in the Radisson Hotel in Miami. We were ten economists in his little bedroom—five orthodox and five heterodox. Fujimori asked, "How do you cope with hyperinflation?" The heterodox side said we should run an econometric model, and in one month we would increase the price of noodles, the next month we would increase the price of oil, and so forth. But I simply told the president that hyperinflation is a cancer and that you must take out that tumor and do it as fast as you can because Peru is dying of cancer. Taking out the tumor requires fiscal and monetary discipline. Moreover, there was terrorism in Peru and we were losing the war against terrorism. The main rebel group, the Shining Path, had 10,000 men and US$60 million a year in income, and it was winning the war against our army of 200,000 men. The military had six German submarines, four ships with missiles, twenty Mirage fighter planes, and they were asking for more money.

The big issue was: How do we enter government and cope with this deficit? Maybe I can contribute by sharing my experiences in coping with the deficit. The theory says to reduce expenditure, increase taxes, and you'll get your act together; the deficit will be reduced. Okay, but how did we do it? In order to reduce the deficit, it's necessary to focus on simple ideas.

We were in hell. For me the definition of hell is terrorism. The Shining Path was controlling more than 50 percent of our territory, and hyperinflation reached almost 8,000 percent a year. That's hell, believe me! The problem is that hell can continue to go down. There is no limit to the number of levels of hell. It's very dynamic.

The first thing we had to do was to deal with the payroll problem, and there were two big aspects that needed to be cut from the beginning. Military salaries were indexed to the salaries of the Senate and the Congress. That meant that when the Senate met, they'd raise their salaries. And because they were the first power of the nation, I couldn't stop them. They would raise their salaries 50 percent or as much as they wanted. Of course, I did not pay them, and they went after me and took me to jail. I was released but I was still trying to withhold the money. The problem was that not only those 500 congressmen were affected but also 300,000 military employees. Every time the congressmen raised their salaries, they raised the salaries of 300,000 military personnel. Thus, my first measure was to switch that indexation.

Let me tell you that you cannot try to convince the military to cut indexation; it's a little bit risky. They really throw you out. So we sent a decree to the president instead of to the Congress—a very important decree, in which the whole military structure was indexed to the president's salary. And of course the president's salary was frozen. Luckily we passed the decree on Friday, and between Friday and Saturday at 5 A.M., their salaries were indexed to the president's salary. The military moved their tanks over the weekend, but they accepted that we were going to be, to an extent, reasonable with the president's salary. That was the first move. Once they swallowed that—and we were alive after that—that was our first step. We had dealt with the situation for 300,000 people. I know they were earning ridiculous salaries after hyperinflation, but that's what hyperinflation means—the bankruptcy of a country.

The second big step was a very simple definition, an important definition, which says that if you don't work one day, you don't get paid that day. It's a biblical definition. If you don't work, you don't eat. Why? Because during the Garcia regime, many people went on strike and they still got paid. Imagine a million public employees going on strike and continuing to be paid. Even though the strike lasted for months, nothing happened. The turning point for the deficit was to cope with the 400,000 teachers that went on strike. The teachers were earning US$150 a month, which was reduced to US$30 because of hyperinflation. It's true that the teachers couldn't survive on US$30 a month—that's one dollar a day—and they asked for a tenfold raise to US$300 a month. Imagine, if you multiply by ten the salaries for the teachers: then come the nurses, the doctors, and then comes the army, and then you have a big, big problem.

So we definitely had to deal with the teachers. The minister of education paid the teachers during the first month of the strike. And that was a bad move. Why should they bother to return to work? So we sent a very clear message saying that we were not going to pay their salaries while they were on strike, and in the second month, we didn't pay. We said we could only pay a raise from US$30 to US$45, not from US$30 to US$300.

The teacher's union was totally controlled by the Shining Path. And, of course, there was a big confrontation with the government. During the first month, 400,000 teachers were marching on the streets, burning cars, and 7 million students were at home. That was the first month. Violence was awful in May 1991. Both the Ministry of Economy and Finance, my ministry, and the Ministry of Education were hit by rockets. They blew out the eleventh floor in the Ministry of Education, and they missed my floor, which was floor number nine, because they hit floor number seven. That was what we had to cope with.

But after one month the teachers realized what fiscal discipline was, and then we negotiated with the Shining Path. Those were tough negotiations. I knew that they couldn't keep the strike going for two or three months; it was impossible for them. Even so, everybody was watching us and everybody was betting against us, betting that we wouldn't get our act together. Thank God the president backed me up. He said, "Go all the way, I'll back you." Thank goodness because, you know, presidents tend to chicken out when you have 7 million students at home and 400,000 teachers marching in the streets.

Nevertheless, the negotiations were not complicated. My meeting with the Sindicato Único de Trabajadores (SUTEP), was a simple one that lasted only fifteen minutes. The first comment was, "Minister, we have you here at the negotiating table?" "Yes, I am here." The second comment was, "Because of your stubbornness we are going to miss the whole academic year." My reply was a short one, a very short one: "Look, for what you have been teaching for the past twenty years, we've been wasting all the academic years." That was tough. And the third exchange was that they were going on an indefinite strike. My reply was, "Look, every month you're on strike I save US$40 million. I need three more months to balance my budget."

Although they left very annoyed, I knew that SUTEP was going to go down and that the whole strike was going to go down. And one month later, the strike was over and there were no more strikes by the teachers' union for five years. We raised their salaries to US$45, which was ridiculous, but that was the only way to get out of hyperinflation. Amazingly, the minute we got the situation with the teachers' union under control, the expectations of all the economic agents started to change. Inflation started to go down from 7.7 percent a month to around 5 percent. It moved slowly due to all the schemes that were in place, but the change was very important.

The other important element was the policemen's Christmas bonus. I ran out of cash on December 24 at 8 P.M. The Banco de la Nación didn't have a single sol. Imagine trying to explain monetary discipline to 80,000 policemen at 8 P.M. on Christmas Eve. So I called my friend at the Central Bank and asked him to lend me some money until Monday. It was a Friday and he said, "Minister Boloña, you are always preaching about monetary discipline. That means that I am not going to give you money to pay salaries." So I had to call big companies and ask them to advance some taxes on Friday night. I could do this because I had moral persuasion with those companies, and they gave me those taxes and I paid the bonus.

On the expenditure side, it was very, very tough. But if we had not controlled expenditure we would have been in deep problems. We also looked at what was going on with pensions. We had 300,000 people receiving US$15 a month as their pension. The whole social security system was bankrupt, but that's the pay-as-you-go scheme. We were really taking advantage of the pensioners because of hyperinflation, but that's how we got into a new scheme. We privatized the pension funds and raised their salary to US$150 a month, and today it may be up to US$200 a month.

In terms of terrorism, the military was asking for US$2 billion to fight terrorism. They wanted to buy ships; they wanted to buy planes; they wanted to buy everything. We said no, that we were going to buy helicopters and machine guns. We also said that we were going to buy shotguns to arm the *ronderos* (that is, self-defense groups formed by *campesinos*). That was also a big decision. The president persuaded us that we should give shotguns to the *ronderos*. He was right because the Shining Path would go into the small towns, take their livestock and their sons, and rob them. This plan worked: it helped with our intelligence, and we started to focus on a different type of war that didn't involve the big toys that the military wanted to buy.

The situation with Ecuador was also a big problem. Ecuador saw that we were in very deep trouble, and they realized that this was the time to wage a war. It was hard for us to get our act together, especially when terrorists were our first enemy. But peace with Ecuador, for me, is a very good thing, and it's going to save each country US$500 million a year. Although peace was achieved later, we still had it very clearly in our minds that we had to cope with military expenditures.

So, really, our deficit, which was 16 percent of GDP, was mainly financed by taxes and by the inflation tax. We had to get our inflation tax down, and that definitely meant reducing expenditures. But we also needed to work on taxation. Taxation was a joke. With tax collections of only 4 percent of GDP, nobody was paying taxes and inflation was eroding our tax base. We had two hundred taxes, and we reduced them to seven in only a few months. We eliminated all earmarked taxes. Incredibly, we realized that we were collecting taxes for the Shining Path. For example, we had taxes on shoe polishers, which were collected by the government and given to the Union of Shoe Polishers. The president of that union was a well-known Shining Path member. The things we were doing were amazing. We simply eliminated a lot of nonsense taxes and concentrated mainly on four important ones. These were the value-added tax, a two-tiered income tax, import duties, and a tax on petrol, beer, and sodas.

Another element of our internal financing was the Central Bank. The Central Bank was directly responsible for several subsidies, which we had to cut in the name of fiscal and monetary discipline. Our four development banks were also increasing the deficit. We had a bank for culture, industry, mining, and construction. And guess what? Every five years they would go bankrupt to the tune of 500 million to a billion dollars. Then the new government would recapitalize them and they'd start the party once again. These banks lent money in a very free manner. We realized that if we really wanted to cut the deficit, we needed to eliminate the development banks, which had around 7,000 employees.

We closed them all in three months. It was very simple. I asked the Central Bank if they wanted to capitalize the banks and they said no. We didn't have the money at the Ministry of Economy and Finance, either, so we just liquidated them. A lot of people in agriculture were very annoyed because these banks maintained their standard of living. They would take out a loan and not repay it, but they also went to Europe and had nice cars and whatever else. They would simply get a congressman to say that the agricultural sector was in a state of emergency and that the loans should be forgiven. That happened every other year, and the same happened in each of the sectors.

Social security, as I mentioned, was a similar story. It was completely bankrupt with a net worth of minus US$20 million. So we simply had to eliminate the pension funds, keep social security as a safety net, and privatize the whole thing.

The other big problem was the public enterprise deficit, which was around 5 percent of GDP. Of course, the required measure was just to privatize everything, but the president was not convinced about it. He allowed us to privatize only twenty firms at first. But afterward we convinced him to privatize all two hundred state-owned enterprises. We took in US$8 billion from privatization and another US$7 billion from new investments. So that was a nice measure that gave us positive results in the short run and started to give good results in the medium term.

The other element for the deficit was the private sector. The private sector, such as it was, exerted big pressure for the government to run a deficit. As liberal economists we were assuming that we had a private sector, and then we realized that what we had was a quasipublic sector. So we had to privatize the private sector. This was a very important measure to keep our deficit under control. What do I mean? In the previous model, profits were privatized but losses were socialized. When they earned money, it was theirs, but when they lost money, the government took care of the losses. There were many other problems with the private sector model. They did not pay taxes, they received subsidized credit, they did not compete, they did not pay back their loans, and they received subsidized public services. This was a very populist model. It was cheaper for us to send them a check at home instead of having them work because it was too expensive for the country. So we had to change the rules by privatizing profits and losses: if you earn a dollar, it's yours; if you lose a dollar, that's your problem. Also, you'll pay your debts, your interest will be a positive, real interest rate, you'll pay your taxes, you'll compete, you don't get to have monopolies, and the prices you pay for public utilities will reflect their costs and scarcity levels. These changes were very important to avoid bigger deficits.

Now, in terms of financing the deficit, the problem was that even though we reduced our deficit to around 2 percent of GDP, we were also paying around 2 percent of GDP for foreign debt service. Remember that we were ineligible to get new loans. So first we had to collect a billion dollars from the Grupo de Apoyo and make the gesture of paying the international financial institutions to start the whole process once again. Then we received loans from the IDB, the World Bank, and the IMF. But we also had to solve some problems with the private banks and then solve the problems with other countries, like the Russians. We applied market economy to our Russian debt. They had loaned us a billion dollars in rubles some twenty years earlier, and we paid them with today's exchange rate. So we only paid them US$100 million.

However, even when we got our act together, meaning that we had achieved a deficit of 2 percent of GDP and expenditures of around 15 percent of our income, temptations would arise. We would ask ourselves: How about using capital markets or issuing sovereign bonds? I didn't want to get into sovereign bonds, except for the Brady bonds that were used to refinance debt. Not new government bonds. I didn't want to do that because it's like an alcoholic who takes a drink. I thought we should show that Peru could function effectively for a couple of decades and then start to use capital markets to finance its fiscal deficits.

So we kept a very simple way of managing our finances. Expenditure was whatever was received as income or as taxes. At most, we would receive maybe 2 percent of GDP in new debt in order to maintain access to international credit markets. And that is how we kept our finances.

Temptations always appear, though, and the biggest temptation that we have had is the political cycle. For his reelection in 1994–95, Fujimori overspent and inflated the economy. We almost went into deep trouble. We ended up with a balance-of-payments deficit. So we had to slow down our economy in 1996. We lost two years inflating the economy and one year stopping the economy because of the political cycle for Fujimori's first reelection.

And now we are in our second political cycle, and Fujimori's cycle is a very short one. It seems that, maybe in four or five months, Fujimori will inflate the economy, and then Peru will pay the bill after his reelection. This is a tough reelection because people are feeling the pinch in their pocket with the current recession. We have not yet learned to cope properly with the political cycle in our country, especially when our government is concentrating power instead of decentralizing power. Instead of making institutional reforms, it has been weakening institutions.

So that's how we dealt with our deficit in Peru, and I think maybe the important part of this story is how to do things. The principles are easy: get expenditures down, get income up, and things will be okay. But the implementation is not easy. The politics of how to do things is important. It's necessary to apply the right phrase at the right moment to convince politicians, to convince the president, to convince the military, to convince congressmen. You need simple ideas that make the right connection at the right moment. And you must be prepared. And sometimes it's necessary to be in really deep trouble to make big changes. Otherwise, you sometimes just don't act.

So that's more or less the experience I wanted to share with you. However, in making these changes, you should be very clear what size your state should be, what size government you want. When we were convincing our president of these changes, we said that the size of the Peruvian government should be around 15 percent of GDP. If the goal is clear, then expenditures can be cut in a very neat way. Keep it simple and avoid getting lost in a lot of details. Our financing was mainly internal because we were not eligible for external financing. Later, when we started to open our economy and get external funds, we only used them to help us with the payment of external debts. We have a debt of 50 percent of GDP, depending on which figure you like to use. Regardless, it's a big debt, and it used to be around 100 percent of GDP. But we reduced it through privatization, concessions, and through other intelligent mechanisms. That's what we should all be aiming for.

Panel Discussion on International Lending and Capital Flows

International Lending and Capital Flows

FRANCISCO GIL-DÍAZ
Avantel

I very much appreciate the invitation to this conference by the Atlanta Fed. After two years in the private sector in the phone business, it is refreshing to be invited again in my capacity as an economist.

The basic argument that I want to present here today is that foreign debt in emerging market countries is public debt. The problem with emerging market governments and emerging market countries is that emerging market debt is, in the end, public debt. This is evident in so far as local hard-currency lending of last resort by central banks or treasuries is leveraged on official outside support, for example through rescues by the U.S. Treasury, the International Monetary Fund (IMF), the World Bank, and the Bank for International Settlements (BIS).

I would like to start with a brief historical perspective, pertinent because the development of international capital markets over the past few years has been surprisingly fast and varied. This evolution has promoted profound changes in the structure of external finance in emerging market countries and increased their reliance on official outside support. This shift may also have enhanced moral hazard.

The capitalization of markets has undergone tremendous growth in recent years, jumping from US\$14 billion to US\$24 billion between 1993 and 1997 (see Chart 1). The rising amount of assets in equity and mutual funds is another change that has been well documented. David Hale (1996) has shown how these assets grew threefold in the five years between 1990 and 1995 (see Chart 2).

The relative positioning of banks vis-à-vis mutual funds is quite different from what it used to be. In 1973 and 1974, rising oil prices triggered a substantial increase in savings by the Arab countries and some other oil-producing countries. International markets started changing because the Arab countries had to find borrowers, and they found ready sovereign borrowers in developing countries, which took out a huge amount of debt. Most of the new debt was channeled through private banks.

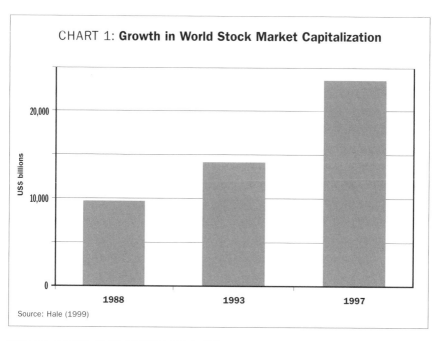

CHART 1: **Growth in World Stock Market Capitalization**

US$ billions

20,000

10,000

0

1988   1993   1997

Source: Hale (1999)

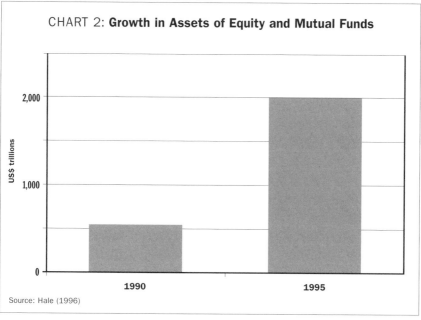

CHART 2: **Growth in Assets of Equity and Mutual Funds**

US$ trillions

2,000

1,000

0

1990   1995

Source: Hale (1996)

Then in the late seventies, U.S. interest rates rose and the debt burden of Latin American countries increased sharply. Since most of our debt was at floating rates, this translated into increased interest payments. Chart 3 shows how interest payments ballooned from 1977 to 1980, after just a few years. These data do not include Eastern Europe and the former Soviet Union, but it is still evident that interest payments rose due to the higher interest rates. There was simply no proportional relation between the growth in interest payments and gross domestic product (GDP) growth in these countries.

In addition to all this debt, it became increasingly hard to borrow internationally for two reasons: the petrodollar bulge ended, and real financial returns improved in home markets when inflation fell in the industrialized world. That was the situation in the eighties. Mexico's debt problems in 1982, after it could no longer service its foreign debt and had nearly exhausted its international reserves, marked the beginning of the contamination type of crisis. In 1982, Mexico was the second-largest emerging market debtor, after Brazil.

There were spillover effects, one of which was of course contamination. Brazil and Argentina became unable to take out additional loans or even to roll over maturing short-term debt. In 1982, Brazil's debt was close to US$88 billion and Argentina's was near US$40 billion. Hundreds of banks had claims

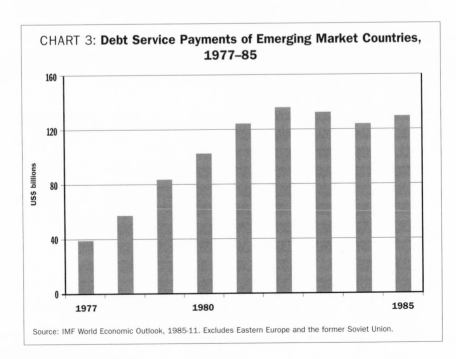

CHART 3: **Debt Service Payments of Emerging Market Countries, 1977–85**

Source: IMF World Economic Outlook, 1985-11. Excludes Eastern Europe and the former Soviet Union.

on Latin America. Giants like Citicorp, Bank of America, and Manufacturers Hanover had loaned the region significant portions of their portfolios.

Then the crisis disappeared and the nineties brought a renewal of capital inflows. One of the reasons for this renewal was the Brady Plan—the ingenious renegotiations of sovereign debt that seemed to dissipate the debt overhang. The decline in U.S. interest rates was also partly responsible for the reawakened interest in the region. But perhaps the greatest incentive to renewed flows was the move in emerging markets towards deregulation, public sector downsizing, trade openness, and stabilization.

Emerging markets and their private sectors were able to leverage those improvements into greater debt. Stock market capitalization in emerging market countries grew from only US$613 billion to US$2.1 trillion from 1990 to 1996. In the industrialized countries, the figure went from $8.8 trillion to US$18.1 trillion during the same period (Hale 1998). These data show the very significant change that allowed emerging markets to leverage their reforms and to acquire significant amounts of private debt.

More recently, Mexico again created a crisis which had a major spillover effect. What were the causes of the 1994 crisis? We have to look again into the behavior of credit and the moral hazard that supported it. The main engine of a smart and sustained increase in demand from leading up to 1994 was a tremendous explosion of credit from development banks and commercial banks. This increase came from banks and from foreign sources. Credit to the private sector rose 270 percent in real terms, just from the local commercial banks in Mexico. But the same type of increase was evident in other sources of credit. A significant portion of that credit was unrecoverable, even without the crisis. The credit expansion did not bring about growth. Instead, the current account became unmanageable and, together with Mexico's fixed exchange rate, culminated in the 1994 crash.

In 1995, the U.S. and Canadian governments, the World Bank, the BIS, and the IMF provided emergency backing that allowed Mexico to emerge from the crisis. This funding led to several new developments in global debt markets. Public and private borrowers are now back in the world debt markets and are relying more on bonds instead of obtaining direct bank credits. Also, because of the lack of a common statistical framework, financial institutions have established research departments all over the world. I would say that in this regard, a serious problem exists in most emerging markets, and it is manifested in the commitments that arose after the recent Asian crisis. Part of this dilemma is that Pete Marwick and all the reputable accounting firms were using lower and differing standards for evaluating institutions in southeast Asian countries and in most of Latin America. So despite the fact that these international accounting firms were auditing and evaluating income statements and balance sheets, they did not provide the transparency and fullness of information or the quality and timely advice that one expects from such firms. International observers simply did not know what was going on in these countries. This lack of transparency and information would, of course, apply to Mexico and most of Latin America.

This situation led international financial institutions to reevaluate their roles. To date, however, they have only proposed common standards and global supervision. Supervisory problems, the absence of accountability, and information problems have provoked international financial institutions, especially the IMF, to look into the definition of common standards and some kind of international supervision.

Notwithstanding the vast and timely amount of new information, the weaning out of the crises, and a new awareness by international official institutions, a large degree of moral hazard remains. We have no indigenous capital markets, only short-term money markets. Panama, which has a dollar economy, is an exception in Latin America. Another one is Chile, where most banking liabilities are dominated in another currency that is neither the dollar nor the Chilean currency but, rather, indexed deposits.

Furthermore, central banks unavoidably continue to be lenders of last resort and commercial banks know they can rely on them. They know they can expect central banks to come to the fore whenever they need them. Development and commercial banks continue to borrow abroad and to lend in the short term in local currency. Therefore a mismatch problem persists because of a lack of domestic capital markets. This has been well documented by Ricardo Hausmann at the Inter-American Development Bank (Hausmann and others 1999). Due to these imbalances and the knowledge that there is a local source of lending of last resort, governments continue to bear responsibility for a country's total indebtedness—not just for the so-called public debt. In turn, governments confide in the ever-present supply of international lending of last resort, which brings us back to the original assertion: all emerging market debt is really public debt.

One could question these concerns based on the ever-present potential for failure derived from moral hazard. After all, emerging market economies have undertaken substantial reforms and public finances have improved. So the question becomes, "Have these reforms solved the problem?" Unfortunately the answer is no, and the foundation for a sustained healthy development is still incomplete. A main reason for this shortcoming is that hidden public debt is substantial.

There are several sources of hidden public debt or of public debt disguised as private debt. Pension liabilities are potentially enormous; not only do pension liabilities exist because of unfunded pension plans at the central government level but there are also huge, unaccounted liabilities. (This is at least true of most state governments in Mexico, and I suspect it is true elsewhere as well.) Though these liabilities are not transparent, they are going to create a tremendous drain on public finances in the next few years.

Then there is the question of development bank debt. We did not follow the healthy example of Carlos Boloña in Peru: we maintained our development bank debt in Mexico. That is true for most of Latin America and other emerging market countries. All kinds of ruses or excuses have been given to maintain development banks. I remember that we took development bank debt out of the definition of public sector debt a few years ago. Incredibly, the IMF allowed this move, and we justified it by saying that we were capitalizing the development banks. But who was capitalizing the development banks? The government! Although government money was injected, evidently it was really just an accounting transaction. We invented the fiction that the development banks were capitalized and thus removed these growing debts from the definition of public sector deficit. I think this was a wrong decision.

In the past few years, ironically, the government deficit has been shown to be greater than the stated figure because development banks' net lending has been negative. But most of their loans remain unrecoverable. Hence it is inexplicable why we persist in leaving development banks out of the assessment of the deficit, but I think the hope is, unfortunately, that these banks will continue to be an instrument of policy in the future. Chart 4 illustrates that Mexican development banks have not been repaying their debts in recent years and thus represent a potential government liability.

There is also public investment disguised as private investment. There are off-budget items that are turnkey projects and are supposed to be self-financed, but the credit risk of these projects ultimately is in the hands of the government. So there is no way to excuse or rationalize putting these items off the budget.

There are other institutional problems in Mexico, like rigid labor laws, which were established in order to have a corporate-type relationship between the labor movement and the government. Furthermore, the lack of regional political competition is a serious problem in most of our countries. Why? Because having a centralized type of government doesn't allow the type of tax collection, expenditure, and regulation at the local level that provides competition among localities. Although this issue hardly

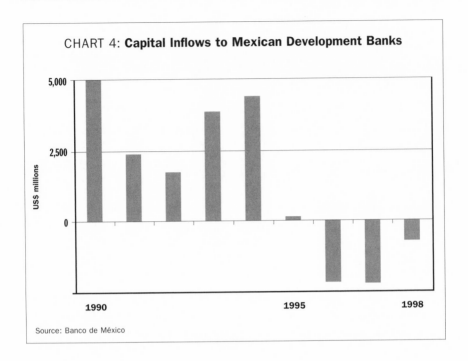

CHART 4: **Capital Inflows to Mexican Development Banks**

Source: Banco de México

ever commands attention, I believe it is one of the most serious forms of backwardness that afflicts us.

General judicial malfunctioning is, of course, another indicator that we have yet to develop a solid base for sustained, healthy development. The courts just don't work. The ability to enforce a contract can depend on connections, bribes, the case reaching the upper, cleaner levels of the courts—or because you are lucky. Or enough time has gone by and it does not really matter who wins because, by then, the contract is worth so little that the victory is pointless.

All these problems may yet explain why Argentina, Brazil, Mexico, and others have not achieved an investment grade credit rating. The lack of local capital markets, the growth of private sector foreign debt, and the resulting asset and liability mismatch, all feed expectations of further pressures on public finances and sustain high real interest rates.

Debt restructuring is becoming more complex, with direct lending decreasing and a growing number of new lenders. This complexity is becoming quite a problem for all the renegotiations; we faced such a problem in 1995. Dispersed lenders do not feel pressured to lend, so even debt rollover becomes complicated. Therein lies the renewed pressure on the official international financial institutions. Greater distance between borrowers and lenders, coupled with the active role of international financial institutions, may be increasing moral hazard instead of diminishing it.

Finally, I would like to conclude by mentioning again that nominal public deficits may hide large debts. We have the central government deficit or the public sector borrowing requirement, but we also have huge off-budget (at least in the case of Mexico) liabilities in development banks. We have financial requirements outside the budget as well. We have the problem of local governments and the problem of financing credit pensions in the future.

Countries that have not tackled their moral hazard problem will face more financing needs. In this environment, medium-sized and small firms will suffer the most because big firms have access to international markets.

To overcome these problems, the development of a common database is necessary for the evaluation of financial instruments. The success of the privatization process and the development of markets will determine financing needs in each country. There is also a need for an enhanced international supervisory role, but it will have to be a private one, not one based on international financial institutions, if it is going to be credible.

References

Banco de México. "Información Financiera y Económica." Available at http://www.banxico.org.mx.

Hale, David. 1996. "Lessons from the Mexican Crisis of 1995 for the Post Cold War International Order." In World Bank (1996).

———. 1998. "Will Emerging Markets Outperform Wall Street after 1998?" Zurich Group (December 9).

———. 1999. "Stock Market Growth and Privatization in Developing Countries." United Nations Conference on Privatization and Regulation (February 16).

Hausmann, Ricardo, Ernesto Stein, Carmen Pagés-Serra, and Michael Gavin. 1999. "Financial Turmoil and Choice of Exchange Rate Regime." Inter-American Development Bank (January).

International Monetary Fund. 1985–91. World Economic Outlook. Washington, D.C.: International Monetary Fund.

United Nations. 1999. Conference on Privatization and Regulation (February).

World Bank. 1996. The World Bank Report on Mexico (February).

International Lending and Capital Flows

In this paper I will not attempt to provide a Wall Street version of the issues that we have been discussing at the seminar on Sustainable Public Sector Finance in Latin America. I am glad that this was not the topic entrusted to me either, since I see very little room for disagreement. I do not mean to trivialize the subject at all by saying merely that budgetary reform is still extremely necessary in most of Latin America, and extremely difficult to achieve. Instead I intend to provide a broad overview of international lending and capital flows, with particular reference to the financing of public sector deficits. I will take advantage of my position towards the end of the schedule, however, to make reference whenever possible to the capital markets issues that arose over the first day and a half of the meeting.

Recent Trends in Capital Flows

There have been important changes in the uses and sources of capital flows around the world over the past couple of years. The Asian crisis has prompted a sharp adjustment in external balances in that region, almost eliminating the current account deficit in emerging markets altogether in 1998 (see Chart 1). Resident net lending and unaccounted outflows remain a significant drain on resources for emerging markets as a whole, despite a drop from US$137 billion in 1998 to an estimated US$90 billion in 1999. In this regard, however, it is important to bear in mind that problems of poor disclosure and data quality, which bedevil accounting practices and fiscal accounts in emerging markets, are particularly acute when it comes to the balance of payments. "Resident net lending and unaccounted outflows," as the Institute for International Finance (IIF) terms it—or capital flight, as is

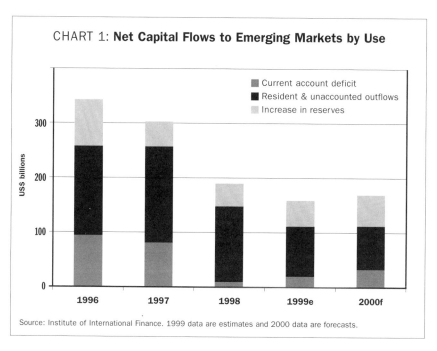

CHART 1: **Net Capital Flows to Emerging Markets by Use**

Legend:
- Current account deficit
- Resident & unaccounted outflows
- Increase in reserves

US$ billions

300, 200, 100, 0

1996 1997 1998 1999e 2000f

Source: Institute of International Finance. 1999 data are estimates and 2000 data are forecasts.

often the case—totaled US$140 billion in Russia in the 1990s, for example, and is still estimated to be running at around US$20 billion a year.

In Latin America, on the other hand, the adjustment has been less dramatic: the region has run down reserves and has continued to post substantial current account deficits (see Chart 2). Capital flight from Latin America appears to be subdued, reflecting well on structural changes during the 1990s and increased domestic confidence in economic prospects.

Capital flows to emerging market countries have also undergone a dramatic transformation in the 1990s and periodically during crises (see Chart 3). Official flows have taken up some of the slack when private sector debt flows have declined. This was particularly the case in Asia in 1997–98 and in Latin America in 1998–99 (see Chart 4). After the liquidity boom of 1996–97, foreign direct investment has resumed the upper hand over portfolio investment as a source of capital for emerging market countries.

Commercial bank credit has contracted for the past two years overall and fell sharply in Latin America in 1999, as we shall see in a moment. Latin America remains the main market for bond issuance as sovereign borrowing needs endure, but corporate issuance has slowed dramatically from the precrisis period in the first half of 1997. This is because companies are shut out by investors who are nervous about the true credit quality of enterprises operating in a deteriorating business environment or because they balk at paying the high financing costs demanded.

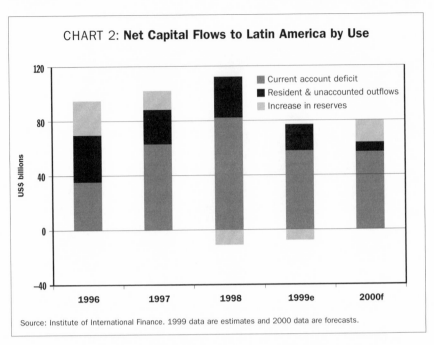

CHART 2: **Net Capital Flows to Latin America by Use**

Legend:
- Current account deficit
- Resident & unaccounted outflows
- Increase in reserves

US$ billions

1996   1997   1998   1999e   2000f

Source: Institute of International Finance. 1999 data are estimates and 2000 data are forecasts.

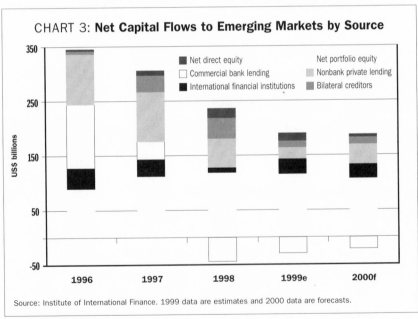

CHART 3: **Net Capital Flows to Emerging Markets by Source**

Legend:
- Net direct equity
- Commercial bank lending
- International financial institutions
- Net portfolio equity
- Nonbank private lending
- Bilateral creditors

US$ billions

1996   1997   1998   1999e   2000f

Source: Institute of International Finance. 1999 data are estimates and 2000 data are forecasts.

A closer look at capital flows to Latin America shows that the region's current account deficit adjusted sharply in 1999 and is expected to stabilize in 2000, after having deteriorated steadily through the mid-1990s as a result of strong domestic demand (especially in post-*real* Brazil) and

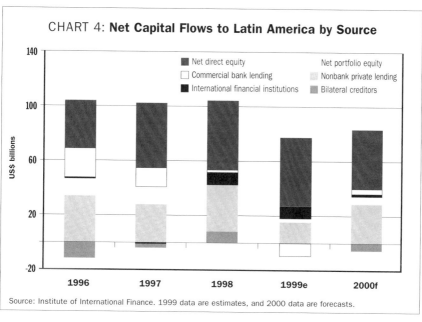

CHART 4: **Net Capital Flows to Latin America by Source**

- Net direct equity
- Commercial bank lending
- International financial institutions
- Net portfolio equity
- Nonbank private lending
- Bilateral creditors

US$ billions

1996   1997   1998   1999e   2000f

Source: Institute of International Finance. 1999 data are estimates, and 2000 data are forecasts.

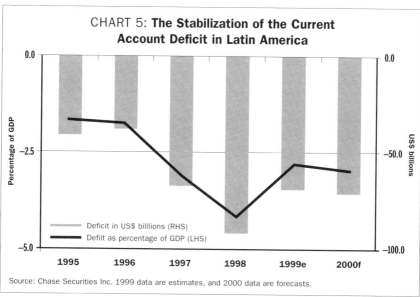

CHART 5: **The Stabilization of the Current Account Deficit in Latin America**

Percentage of GDP

US$ billions

- Deficit in US$ billlions (RHS)
- Defiit as percentage of GDP (LHS)

1995   1996   1997   1998   1999e   2000f

Source: Chase Securities Inc. 1999 data are estimates, and 2000 data are forecasts.

trade liberalization (see Chart 5). Despite shocks to confidence in the region, net private flows are still expected to provide more than enough finance for the current account deficit through the present postcrisis malaise (see Chart 6).

It is worth noting, however, that in the boom years of 1996–97 net private inflows were equivalent to more than double the sum of the region's current

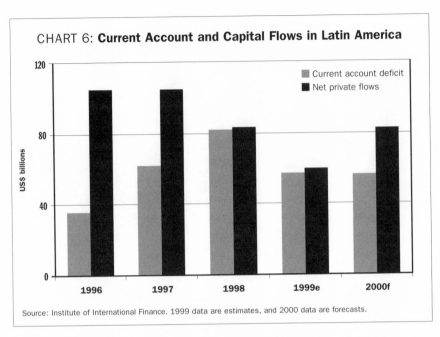

CHART 6: **Current Account and Capital Flows in Latin America**

Source: Institute of International Finance. 1999 data are estimates, and 2000 data are forecasts.

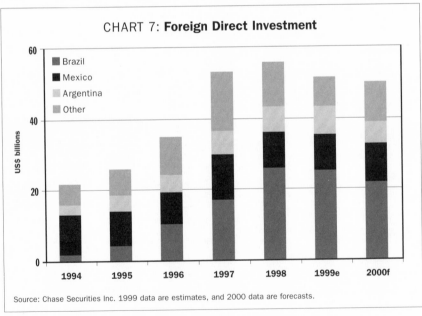

CHART 7: **Foreign Direct Investment**

Source: Chase Securities Inc. 1999 data are estimates, and 2000 data are forecasts.

account deficits. The persistence of strong flows of private capital to the region does suggest that the economic policies pursued both in the run-up to and during the 1998–99 crisis, buttressed by solid multilateral support for such orthodox responses, have helped to maintain the confidence of foreign investors in the future of Latin America. Within the private flows category,

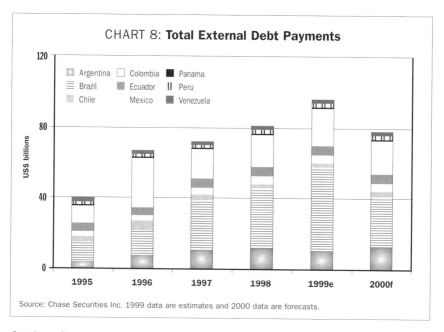

CHART 8: **Total External Debt Payments**

Source: Chase Securities Inc. 1999 data are estimates and 2000 data are forecasts.

foreign direct investment has proved particularly stable (see Chart 7), although a modest decline is expected for 1999–2000 as the privatization schedule tapers off, as Fábio de Oliveira Barbosa mentioned earlier.

The other component of the region's financing needs, namely, external debt amortizations, is playing against Latin America this year, however (see Chart 8). Total amortizations have been rising steadily and are set to peak in 1999 for two main reasons. On the one hand, the grace periods for Brady debt renegotiated in the late 1980s and early 1990s are gradually expiring; on the other hand the two- to three-year corporate loans and bonds extended and issued in 1996–97, when global liquidity was at a peak, are now falling due.

We have already seen how foreign direct investment, which is closely linked to the current account deficit and ideally provides much of its financing, is holding up well in Latin America. The same is not true of private debt-creating flows such as commercial bank lending and bond issuance. Starting in the first quarter of 1998, when it became clear that the region was not going to escape contagion from the devaluations and financial turmoil in Southeast Asia, commercial bank lending fell sharply (see Charts 9 and 10).

This phenomenon is particularly interesting in the case of Brazil, as seen in the previous two charts. You will remember that senior international bankers, occasionally under the auspices of the IIF, were prevailed upon to publicly support the multilateral assistance package for Brazil in the last quarter of 1998 and then the Brazilian government's attempts to stabilize the economy in the wake of the devaluation of the *real* in January

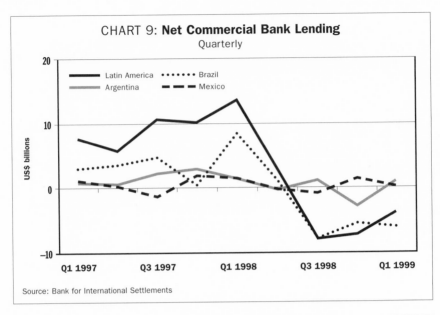

CHART 9: Net Commercial Bank Lending
Quarterly

Source: Bank for International Settlements

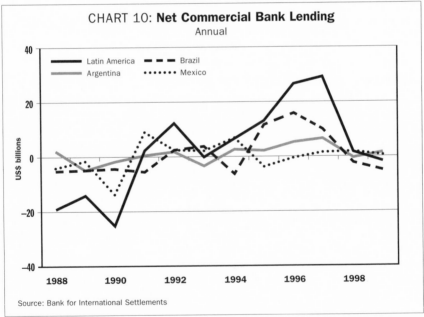

CHART 10: Net Commercial Bank Lending
Annual

Source: Bank for International Settlements

1999. The banks pledged to roll over their lending to Brazil, particularly in the shape of trade lines, and it is possible that this contribution helped to keep the hot topic of involuntary private sector bail-ins off the table at the time.[2] Certainly G7 and multilateral representatives have been heard since to laud the initiative as a worthy example of a private sector contribution to crisis resolution.

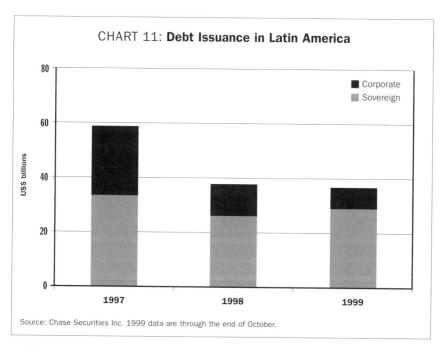

CHART 11: **Debt Issuance in Latin America**

Source: Chase Securities Inc. 1999 data are through the end of October.

The data suggest, however, that bank exposure was not maintained at historic levels. In fact, it appears that the offer or pledge was made once the international banks had already scaled back their lending to Brazil and Argentina, in particular, through net outflows in the third and fourth quarters of 1998. The commitment to maintain credit lines going forward was therefore made from a low base in late 1998. It further appears that those credit lines that were maintained were available largely to big exporters and certainly not to the riskier small and medium-sized enterprises.

This feature of bank lending in Brazil in part explains the absence of a strong V-shaped trade recovery in the wake of the devaluation, since export credit was not available for those smaller companies that might easily have reoriented their production to external markets. Other factors, such as poor export infrastructure and the weakness of demand in neighboring countries, also clearly played a role, of course.

Bond issuance likewise fell sharply with the onset of the Asian crisis and its associated contagion effects (see Chart 11). Sovereign issuance only declined by around US$5 to US$6 billion from 1997 to 1998–99, but corporate issuance was hit particularly hard. This was in part because sovereign needs are more rigid, so governments are forced to accept higher borrowing costs to finance (higher cyclical) deficits; companies, on the other hand, can delay expansion plans or seek equity injections instead. Governments also have more opportunities to diversify their sources of bond financing, by tapping the retail investor base in Europe, for example, which, though it might not be familiar with Latin corporations, would have heard of Argentina. Governments can also diversify by securing multilateral guarantees for a bond issue, as Argentina did in October 1999.

Having examined the major trends in capital flows, the paper will now review some of the developments influencing the borrowing and lending communities in the Latin American debt market.

Evolution of the Borrowers

Changes in the regional and global environment have strongly affected the prospects for international lending and capital flows. Flows to emerging markets fluctuate with global market conditions, as we have just seen, but are also of course vulnerable to specific events in emerging markets. The improvement in sovereign credits through the 1990s has played a crucial role in attracting flows back to Latin America in particular, after lenders were left with severely burnt fingers in the regional debt crisis of 1982.

Reforms in three key areas have contributed to the improvement in sovereign credits:

- *Public Sector Reforms*: Tax and public sector administration reforms to simplify civil service structures and to reduce evasion; deregulation, elimination of subsidies and price controls; privatization of state enterprises and reduction of the public sector deficit; and social security and pension system reforms.
- *External Sector Reforms*: Unification of foreign exchange rates and elimination of foreign exchange controls; simplification of import tariffs, quotas, and export procedures; and liberalization of foreign investment regulations.
- *Financial Sector Reforms*: Liberalization of interest rates and credit controls; reduction of domestic credit subsidies; liberalization of domestic capital markets, privatization of state banks; and foreign participation in financial services.

The first area—public sector reforms—has of course been the focus of our meetings here in Atlanta. Every speaker has touched on some aspect of the reforms listed above. A theme running through that area and the other two, however, is simplification, and this has a specific relevance to the field of capital markets. Carlos Boloña mentioned cuts in the number of taxes imposed in Peru, and there are clearly administrative gains available from simplifying taxation structures. In pursuing this path, however, a government is also making it easier for the investment board or portfolio manager of a pension fund, for example, to follow the fiscal performance of the country. An investor who understands the credit risk in a given country is more likely to follow through with an investment, either by purchasing a new issue or by bidding up the price of a bond in the secondary market.

This process of reform and structural adjustment has been motivated primarily by the lessons of the 1980s. In Latin America's case, the policy agenda of the 1990s conformed fairly closely to the so-called Washington Consensus, which emerged as multilateral lenders in particular drew a reduced set of conclusions from those broad lessons. The resulting policy framework, as adopted in Latin America, had three key elements that feed back into the question of sustainable public sector finance: (1) Countries' inability to pay primarily reflects fiscal problems, not balance-of-payments problems. (2) Capital flight was a major factor in the failure of governments to stabilize their economies in the 1980s, and it usually reflected a lack of confidence in the government's ability to meet its fiscal obligations, leading to fears of monetization and asset seizure (if not the actual event). (3) Finally, resolution of a fundamental fiscal imbalance is a domestic challenge and cannot be secured through increased external "support."

This last point was illustrated by the failure of successive attempts to attract new lending from the private sector during the 1980s, as a result of the inadequacy of fiscal adjustment efforts in Latin America. Multilateral and bilateral lenders were instead forced to provide financing (often through the buildup of arrears) while the private sector waited for indications that the underlying credit quality was improving. Mexico's successful Brady Plan in 1989, for example, which did finally bring in new money, was preceded by several years of impressive fiscal performance.

For many investors, the same fundamental problems and fears lay behind the most recent emerging market scares in Russia and Brazil, which can be classified as classic debt traps even though prompt action by the authorities saved Brazil from the worst-case scenarios painted by many in January 1999 after the devaluation of the *real*. In both cases, hikes in domestic interest rates (to defend currencies) compounded the government's fiscal problem by producing an explosion in the domestic debt, which undermined the sovereign's ability to pay. At this point in the story, the Russian government defaulted on its obligations and Brazil suffered downgrades from ratings agencies. The next stage in the classic debt trap, which materialized with a vengeance in Russia but proved subdued in

Brazil, is that high interest costs lead to recession, which in turn impedes the rest of the economy's ability to pay, thus depressing fiscal revenues and prompting pressure for bailouts.

As we saw earlier, these developments provoked severe capital flight in Russia. Although the support package sponsored by the International Monetary Fund (IMF) has reduced capital flight in Brazil, questions remain concerning the country's ability to address its fiscal problems over the longer term and its capacity to reduce interest rates to sustainable levels.[3] Capital flight remains a major threat for the Brazilian authorities since the much-vaunted ability of the local market to finance most of the government's borrowing needs depends on continued confidence in the domestic financial system. Meanwhile, neighboring Argentina remains the most highly indebted large country in Latin America but is only gradually able to resort to the fledgling domestic market to satisfy financing needs. At times of external volatility, doubt over the government's ability to refinance obligations will rear its head again.

While the governments of Latin America have adopted a new policy framework in response to the lessons of the 1980s, the external environment has not stood still. In particular, the international financial world of the 1990s is fundamentally different from that of the previous decade, demanding even higher standards of prudential control from both the public and private sectors. In a world of securitized finance, money moves quickly and often in huge amounts; this puts a premium on building "cushions" to absorb such swings and on keeping economic performance in line. Likewise, domestic banks are exposed to new risks, including volatility in asset prices and hence in their mark-to-market valuation. An institution's ability to access capital markets may also fluctuate, often constrained by the investor's perception of the sovereign government of the bank's resident country. Against this backdrop of volatility and recurrent emerging market crises, investors' perceptions of the current system's stability have been tested by the evident inability of the IMF and major G-7 powers to dampen risk in the global economy.

Through all the changes, however, there are important elements of the puzzle that endure and are sometimes overlooked both in the frenzy of financial market contagion and in the search for scapegoats after a crisis. One of the most important is the fact that the traditional framework for sovereign credit analysis still holds, and it remains the "bread and butter" of the work of portfolio managers, research analysts, and credit strategists— on Wall Street and around the world. The two pillars for this analysis are a government's willingness and ability to pay (see Box 1). Kurt Weyland yesterday expressed concern over the so-called efficiency of a capital market

---

Box 1: The Determinants of Sovereign Credit Assessment

Willingness to Pay

- Commitment to the reform process
- Ongoing need for capital market access (both sovereign and corporate)
- More onerous legal consequences of defaults on sovereign debt

Ability to Pay

- Economic growth prospects
- GDP, investment, productivity, savings
- Fiscal cash flows and balance sheet
- Budget balance and debt service ratios
- Domestic-plus-external-debt ratio to GDP
- Level of foreign currency reserves

---

response at times of contagion, when it appears that investors are unable to differentiate between good and bad credits. Unfortunately it seems to me that this contagion arises precisely because market participants are engaging in traditional credit analysis and responding to fears that tight liquidity will jeopardize the ability to pay of a wide range of creditors in emerging markets. The effect of this group conclusion is intensified by the safety factor built into those credit decisions to allow for the margin of error in second-guessing the conclusions drawn by other players.

Evolution of the Lenders

Finally, I would like to provide a brief, analytical chronology of the development of the Latin American debt market and to highlight the evolution of perceptions of Latin American debt by U.S. investors. Essentially, changes in the U.S. investor base for emerging market debt can be divided into six stages.

Stage 1: The Pre-Brady Era (before 1993). The marketplace for emerging market debt evolved very slowly in the wake of the 1982 debt crisis. Over its first decade it was characterized mainly by interbank loan swapping and some limited secondary market trading of loans. The market was dominated by the banks themselves, which had large inventories of nonperforming or low-yielding debt as a result of the 1982 defaults and restructurings as well as by dealers, hedge funds, and a few specialist mutual funds. A thumbnail sketch of the market would depict shrewd investors looking to buy undervalued securities from skittish original lenders searching for a way out of the emerging market debt business. As the U.S. Treasury in particular took an interest in organizing a more sustainable solution for the troubled borrowers and a more permanent market for the debt instruments, the Brady plan was born.

Stage 2: The Boom Period (January 1993–February 1994). As more Brady deals were concluded, more players were attracted to the secondary market and liquidity improved. At the same time, improving fundamentals spurred renewed interest in emerging markets as the policy lessons of the 1980s were applied. In terms of the technical characteristics driving the market, the rally in developed country bond markets compressed yields and encouraged fixed-income investors to search further afield for juicy returns (effectively a "flight *from* quality"). The steep U.S. yield curve, with short rates at around just 3 percent, added extra fuel to this heady mix. It was temporarily possible for investors to profit from a carry trade, borrowing in the short term to make leveraged investments in long bonds that included the newly created Brady instruments.

Stage 3: The Impact of Five Fed Hikes (February 1994–June 1995). It quickly seemed that the boom had been premature. The U.S. Federal Reserve started to raise rates in February 1994, prompting drops in all bond markets. Speculative markets such as the infant Brady bond market fell further. Tighter global liquidity exposed the weaknesses of Mexico's financing strategy, which relied on dollar-linked, short-term domestic debt, forcing first the devaluation of the peso in December 1994 and then domestic liquidity crises in both Mexico and Argentina. The latter was seen as particularly vulnerable due to its currency board-style arrangement and weak financial sector. To varying degrees, international assistance and disciplined domestic policy choices were required to prevent more extensive damage to emerging markets in general and the financial systems of those countries in particular.

Stage 4: A Diversified Investor Base Emerges (June 1995–June 1997). Credit fundamentals stabilized slowly after the Federal Reserve's round of tightening and the steadying of the Mexican economy. Crucially, new investors started to enter the emerging debt market, including the long-awaited crossover buyers who augured greater integration with other credit spread markets. This development was interpreted as reducing sensitivity to U.S. interest rates, while helping to ensure that small sell-offs would be contained rather than mushrooming into precipitous declines, as buy-and-hold investors contributed to a sense that the debt was somehow in "firm hands." Meanwhile emerging market credit fundamentals were back on an improving path: Mexico and Argentina recovered quickly, Brazil maintained its impressive trajectory in the wake of the 1994 stabilization plan, and Southeast Asia continued to boom. Against this backdrop, spreads tightened and yields converged around the world. A host of countries in Latin America were able to issue thirty-year bonds, including Argentina, Mexico, Panama, and Venezuela. In June 1997, for example, Brazil was able to issue thirty-year debt at just 395 basis points over U.S. Treasuries. Likewise, a Chilean electricity utility issued 100-year paper. With hindsight such issues look like clear evidence of euphoria, but at the time they seemed rational bets on the future prospects of developing countries in a liberalizing global economy.

Stage 5: All Bets are Off (July 1997–March 1999). Just when it seemed that the good times were there to stay, the next crisis emerged from an unexpected source. The devaluation of the Thai baht in July 1997 precipitated a series of Asian currency crises, which spread to the external debt markets of a wide range of developing countries in October 1997. The greater leverage at work in the market contributed to a far greater level of contagion than during the 1995 Tequila Crisis. Over an extended period, asset prices suffered extreme volatility across all sectors of emerging market debt, capped by extraordinary losses in Russia in August 1998. The pessimism at international financial gatherings was palpable, as new questions were raised by the crisis about the viability of emerging market debt as an asset class. In a more overt illustration that recovery value was overtaking the probability of default as a benchmark, the bonds of several countries started to trade on price rather than on a spread basis. The crisis itself also had its own victims. The rating agencies of course responded to the deterioration in sovereign creditworthiness with a wave of successive ratings downgrades, and the extended downturn forced speculative investors out of the market. The resulting lack of liquidity, at a time of heightened market stress, in turn further exacerbated other losses as well as reinforced the pessimism weighing on the asset class.

Stage 6: So Far, So Good (March 1999 to the present). After two disastrous years for emerging market fixed-income investors, 1999 finally turned out to offer some reward for those who stuck to their guns. Wider spreads offered attractive entry points for new investors, and technical factors in the market were broadly supportive since leveraged investors had largely been forced out. On the other hand, the very poor performance of dedicated emerging market funds in 1997–98 meant that very little new cash flowed to this kind of institutional investor. Instead, the marginal bid for the emerging market asset class came increasingly from high-grade investors with relatively lower risk tolerance who were looking to gain modest yield enhancement by dipping their toes into emerging market debt. These investors are known as "crossover" investors.

In order to focus this overview of international lending and capital inflows back onto the question of sustainable public sector finance in Latin America, it is worth drawing just a couple of conclusions from the gyrations in the emerging market debt universe in the second half of the 1990s. There are two important implications of this shifting investor base. First, it is worth bearing in mind that while varying degrees of leverage in the market can accentuate or dampen the contagion effects of financial crises, the ultimate focus of the institutional investor remains on traditional credit analysis reflecting the sovereign debtors' willingness and ability to pay. This is particularly the case for so-called crossover investors who are forced to draw a sharp distinction between high-grade issues and non-investment-grade issues. The importance of sustainable public sector finance therefore extends beyond its inherent value for the country in and of itself and into financing costs for the government, which in turn helps to create a virtuous circle where the reward for good behavior in reducing noninterest expenditure, for example, is a further reduction in interest costs.

The second lesson at first glance appears to be a harsher one, however, in that no obvious remedy is at hand. The greater differentiation between those sovereign issuers that can attract crossover investors and those that cannot will condemn governments with weak public finances to alternative sources of funding. In the absence of developed local financial markets, this often means running arrears on payments to suppliers or on wages to public sector employees. Such a strategy undermines economic activity and is not sustainable, as Ecuador's government discovered in the summer of 1999 (see Box 2). On the other hand, it is really only the legacy of those heady days of early 1997 that suggests that developing country governments are somehow entitled to tap international capital markets to fund budget deficits, and a dose of a harsher reality in this regard may also be the discipline necessary to push the more recalcitrant administrations in the direction of the reforms and improvements discussed at this conference.

Box 2: Outline of a Case Study of Peru and Ecuador

The contrasting fortunes of two Andean neighbors may offer a useful illustration of how international lending and capital flows can be a double-edged sword for potential borrowers. The divergent paths of Peru and Ecuador during the 1990s certainly show how investor perceptions can shift rapidly.

The following is a thumbnail sketch of events over the period. This outline could serve as the basis for a deeper exploration of the political and economic dynamics underlying the varying fortunes of the two countries.

- Both countries suffered heavily in the 1980s, with Peru's domestic political condition attracting more headlines and unorthodox "solutions" exacerbating the problems.

- Both countries entered the 1990s with large, unresolved arrears on commercial bank debt and Paris Club debt. Peru was suffering from hyperinflation.

- Sweeping reform in Peru and modest effort in Ecuador facilitated Brady agreements and Paris Club restructuring.

- Peru maintained an austere fiscal stance throughout the decade, recovering in a very disciplined way from the temporary deterioration of the 1994–95 electoral cycle; Ecuador failed to reform budgetary or broader economic institutions but took advantage of abundant global liquidity to finance fiscal deficits. Ecuador appears to be stuck in a permanent cycle of political instability.

The contrast between the two has been evident not only in their fiscal stance but also in their approach to international capital markets: Peru has so far resisted the temptation to borrow even when resources were available, but Ecuador rushed to market in 1997. Currently, Peru is steadily buying back Brady debt to improve its external ratios while Ecuador is once again in default and faces complex legal wrangles.

Notes

1 The views presented here are those of the author and are not necessarily those of Chase Securities Inc.

2 Private sector bail-ins generally refer to the idea that private bondholders should shoulder part of the burden in sovereign debt restructurings.

3 These concerns have eased somewhat in the period since the Atlanta conference with the passage through Congress of important fiscal legislation, including private sector social security reform, the Fiscal Responsibility Law, and the revised Fiscal Stabilization Fund.

Comments

ROBERT EISENBEIS
Federal Reserve Bank of Atlanta

Thank you very much. I'd like to take this opportunity to thank you all again for coming and participating in this conference. I think it has been a very interesting meeting and one that has delivered many important insights about what some of the current problems are and what possible solutions are available.

I'd like to take a few minutes to reflect upon a number of the points that both Francisco and Graham made as those insights relate to the development of financial markets and capital flows. I find very little to disagree with in terms of the key ideas that they present, so rather than concentrate on the specifics, I'd like to discuss a number of observations they put forward, to see where this takes us. And, in the time we have left, I'd like to throw out some ideas for discussion.

First, I'd like to build on the point that Graham made with regard to the evolution of financial markets. The international financial system is evolving, and it's evolving at a very rapid rate. When one can talk about six stages in a matter of just ten years, as Graham did, that tells something about how fast things are evolving and changing. They are evolving and changing in several different ways. First of all, markets are becoming larger. That is pretty clear, and the data have been well documented. Second, they are becoming more informed and more efficient than they've ever been before. Third, we are seeing an evolution away from financial institutions, and particularly commercial banks, serving as primary sources of funding to a greater reliance on capital markets. Debt issuance is becoming a major source of funds. That's something we see here in the United States as well. It's a logical consequence of the greater efficiency of markets as a whole. And following from this consequence come interesting generalizations.

One generalization is that, for all practical purposes, the era of the free lunch in terms of access to cheap money is essentially gone, or almost gone. What I mean by this is that we had somewhat of a free lunch back in the 1970s when we were recycling the petrodollars and there was an abundance of funds. Lenders were not very informed, and, although they thought they were diversified, they did not realize that any country that is dependent upon oil is also dependent on the price of oil. It doesn't make any difference where lenders are lending—if repayments are dependent on the price of oil, lenders are not diversified. Another aspect of the free lunch that I think is gone pertains to the world of efficient capital markets: in this environment it's not possible to sustain any sort of fiscal deficit for a protracted period of time without incurring some kind of cost. This is especially true in Latin America today, and it's something we have all discussed over the last day and a half.

Talking about financing fiscal deficits is almost a non sequitur in the context of efficient and global capital markets. A country cannot continue to borrow in excess of its revenues on a sustainable basis. Market discipline is going to become a daily fact of life for governments as they try to manage their fiscal situations.

This affects the core of the political, social, and cultural fabric that has been supported in some of the Latin American countries. It goes to the very heart of how many of these countries have been run for years. It is hard, I believe, to run an economy—or society for that matter—without a well-functioning legal system. And the less developed a country's legal system, the more the market is ultimately going to penalize that inefficiency.

Fiscal disciplines apply not only at the federal level but also at the state and local levels—and I think Brazil is a case in point. It's not enough to fix the fiscal problems at the federal level alone without also getting things together at the state and local levels. There is going to be a lot of difficulty as people try to deal with the need for reforms. Again, however, problems at the local level are, I think, a logical consequence of the pressure that well-developed financial markets are going to put on countries. It means that government won't be able to maintain unsustainable monetary policies or fiscal policies over a protracted period of time without suffering certain kinds of difficulties.

In many ways, the current situation in Latin America can be seen as a triage situation. One example is what we heard this morning about Peru, which faced a very difficult set of circumstances and had to try to begin to put policies in place that would remedy the situation quickly. Triage is different from plans developed to respond to the fiscal sustainability question in the longer haul or from evolution forced gradually by markets.

The International Monetary Fund has largely been engaged in triage situations as well. But over the longer haul, are they going to be able to continue to engage in those kinds of activities without engendering the moral hazard problem that Francisco talked about? This is a very real question, and one that is going to have to be dealt with in the longer run. It remains on the table for the international community to come to grips with in one way or another.

Another point I'd like to make deals with the question of coping with so-called capital flight. There were some discussions earlier of how volatile markets have become. I have a somewhat different view as I assess and reflect upon what happened in Asia compared with Latin America. I think in the Asian situation, capital actually responded modestly over a long period of time and on a relatively gradual basis. I guess whether you think it was gradual or not depends upon which side of the Pacific you are on. But the fact of the matter is that all the money did not come out overnight; it came out on a gradual basis over several months. A similar kind of thing happened in Latin America. Initially everybody seemed to be hit with the same risk spread, but investors started to learn, and the markets again continued this evolution process. A balancing of spreads and a differentiation of spreads became apparent, depending upon what the underlying fiscal and financial situation was in individual countries. So, the spreads opened up and lenders started differentiating even more among countries quickly. Thus I think it's an overexaggeration to say that everybody was painted with the same brush in that crisis. I don't think the evidence supports that. And this distinction among countries is a trend that is going to continue.

The last point I'd like to make also pertains to the issue of capital flight and has to do with the sorts of policies that can be put into place to try to insulate the domestic economy from what's going on in the rest of the world. I'd like to submit that it's going to be difficult to do that. And I'd like to look at Chile for just a second. Everybody has been holding up capital controls as a model of the way to try to deal with the short-term situation. It clearly is a short-term situation and, if you believe in the efficiency and effective functioning of global capital markets, it seems obvious that Chile will not be able to sustain those restrictions on short-term capital flows. Institutions will find ways around those controls, or else funds will leave the country. And in the meantime, the controls will increase the costs of investment in those maturities for which the controls are in place as well as introduce distortions into the functioning of their financial markets.

The bottom line is that market discipline is pervasive: it will continue to work and evolve along the lines that it has thus far. It's very difficult for countries to operate in this kind of evolving environment because we don't know how quickly markets and market instruments will change. This uncertainty doubles the problem for those in a policy-making position. But I am optimistic about the impact that market discipline will have. It may signal an end to the horrendous costs of repeated financial crises resulting from the unsustainable policies that have been put in place in the past in many developing countries. Obviously, we will see a greater freedom for individuals as markets work. So I am pretty optimistic. It may be difficult to deal with the transition, but that's what most of us here are involved with, and plotting the right course is key to a successful policy.

Speeches

Prospects and Dilemmas for Sustainable Social Sector Funding in Latin America

ANN HELWEGE[1]

Tufts University

Since 1990, there has been a change in the tenor of discussions about social policy in Latin America. Poverty and inequality are no longer relegated to the last chapter of the book. In fact, a vast literature has emerged on the causes of poverty, the virtuous circle between redistribution and growth, and the design of policies to target the poor effectively. The World Bank has adopted the banner "A World without Poverty" and has made its bailouts contingent on the funding of social programs. The impression one gets is that there is a consensus on the need to reduce poverty.

Does this consensus have a Latin American counterpart? Certainly the rhetoric has changed. And there are highly visible changes in policy: more money has been allocated to primary schools, innovative food and credit programs have replaced broad subsidies, expensive pension plans have been overhauled, and private firms now provide basic services like water supply. But do these changes reflect a significant shift in social sector priorities in favor of the poor?

The overall poverty rate remains above that which prevailed before the debt crisis, and roughly 150 million Latin Americans live on less than $2 per day. The task of overcoming poverty is now Herculean: strong macroeconomic growth has proven a feeble remedy, and we now no longer have that. Budgets are tight and governments that can articulate effective social agendas are not necessarily able to finance them. In most countries, the poor remain politically weak and unable to drive social agendas through the power of the vote. Has enthusiasm for more effective targeting faltered in the face of political reality?

Today I intend to share preliminary results of work with Eliana Cardoso on changes in social policy in Argentina, Brazil, and Mexico in the 1990s. We asked: How extensively have social policies actually changed? How have the overall level of spending and its composition changed? Do social policies now reflect the new paradigm of better targeting?

Trends in the 1990s

Social spending rose significantly in Latin America during the 1990s.[2] According to the United Nations, per capita social expenditure rose from $331 in 1990–91 to $457 in 1996–97, an increase of 38 percent (United Nations 1999). Gains were evident in nearly every country in the region: in Peru, Paraguay, Bolivia, and Colombia, social spending nearly doubled. There has also been a regional trend toward increased social expenditure as a percent of government spending. For example, in Argentina, the share of social expenditures in total fiscal expenditures rose from 50 percent in 1980 to 65 percent in 1997.

That's the good news. The bad news is that this positive trend reflects the highly procyclical nature of social spending.[3] The relationship between growth and social expenditure is clear in the case of Argentina

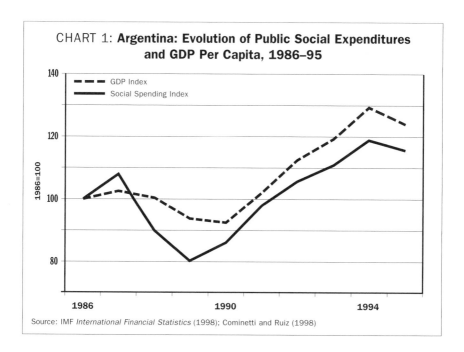

CHART 1: **Argentina: Evolution of Public Social Expenditures and GDP Per Capita, 1986–95**

- - - GDP Index
—— Social Spending Index

Source: IMF *International Financial Statistics* (1998); Cominetti and Ruiz (1998) (see Chart 1). Not only does social spending tend to rise and fall with gross domestic product (GDP) but the amplitude of these swings is accentuated by the fact that social spending tends to fall proportionately more than GDP in a recession. Government spending may help to redress "social deficits" after a crisis, but the patterns observed here suggest it exacerbates the effect of the crisis itself on the poor. Thus the slowdown in regional growth observed in 1999 threatens to undermine progress achieved since 1990.

The Composition of Social Expenditure

By far the largest social expenditure category in all three countries is social security and pensions. It consumes nearly half of total social expenditures in Argentina and Brazil. Health and education are the other two large categories while housing and water and sanitation are minor.

The relative shares of the different categories have remained fairly constant in the past decade (see Tables 1 and 2). In other words, there has been no significant change in the focus of social expenditure policy. Rising overall expenditures have supported an absolute expansion of spending in most areas, but this should not be confused with a change in social sector priorities.

Thus we must ask: How well does the existing structure of social spending serve the needs of the poor? If Latin Americans are not changing the composition of social spending, are they doing a better job of targeting the resources within these sectors to the poor?

Social Security. In the United States, Social Security evolved as an antipoverty program, and its expansion has meant that the elderly are no longer so disproportionately poor. The distributional benefits of Latin American social security systems have been much more limited; they are typically regressive. In Brazil, for example, the poorest 37 percent of the nation's population received only 9 percent of social security benefits in 1990 while the top 27 percent garnered 42 percent.[4]

Several countries in the region have undertaken pension reform, but the results vary greatly. Prior to reform, most Latin American countries relied on a pay-as-you-go system, with no connection between benefits and contributions. Moreover, entitlement rules encouraged evasion and fraud. Under conditions of high inflation, governments could easily make generous promises to future pensioners. With the end of inflation, the huge deficits proved unsustainable.

TABLE 1: **Argentina: Public Social Expenditures by Categories**
(Percent of Total Social Expenditures)

	1980–89	1990—97
Social Security and Pensions	46.8	48.0
Health Expenditure	27.6	27.8
Education Expenditure	19.2	20.2
Housing Expenditure	4.8	3.0
Expenditures for Water and Sanitation	1.5	1.0

Source: Author's calculations based on data from the government of Argentina's Secretariat of Economic and Regional Planning (1998)

TABLE 2: **Brazil: Social Expenditures by All Levels of Government**
(As a Share of GDP)

	1994	1996
Total	20.2	20.9
Education	4.2	4.2
Health	3.3	3.2
Social Security and Benefits to Civil Servants	9.3	10.3
Food and Social Assistance	0.7	0.6
Regional and Urban Development	1.7	1.7
Others	1.0	0.9

Sources: Brazilian Secretariat of the National Treasury/Federal Data Processing Service for Federal Government, Brazilian Institute of Geography and Statistics/Department of National Accounts (IBGE/DECNA) for States and Municipalities, and the Institute of Applied Economic Research (IPEA), *Gasto Social das Tres Esferas de Governo*, Rio de Janeiro (1999)

The old systems were inexcusably inefficient, and they did little to help the poor. They arguably offered a built-in system of implicit subsidies from high-earning workers to low-income workers in the formal sector, but they functioned ineptly even in this realm. Governments have undertaken social security reform not just for the fiscal payoff but as a signal to international financial markets that they can successfully tackle big problems. How good are the reforms?

A common model has been a shift toward privately managed individual accounts like those implemented in Chile more than a decade ago.[5] These market-oriented, private pension schemes are typically complemented by a safety net for the lowest income workers and older workers who are close to retirement. Argentina, Mexico, and Peru have adopted variations on this theme. Brazil has made only minimal headway in its reforms.

So far, most workers are opting for individual accounts: two-thirds of contributors in Argentina shifted to individual accounts within the first three years. Since a reform was enacted in 1997, 15 million Mexicans have moved to private schemes despite the fact that the Mexican plan requires substantial investment in questionable government securities. The trend certainly extracts the government from part of its responsibility to care for the aging middle class. In the long run, this has the potential to save vast sums of money.

From a targeting point of view, the gains are less obvious. The new private schemes eliminate redistribution between high- and low-income workers in the formal sector, and the benefits offered to those who stay in the publicly funded schemes are minimal. In Argentina, for example, the minimum pension is just 27.5 percent of the average wage earned prior to retirement, provided contributions have been paid for thirty years. Women, who spend less time in the labor force, are unlikely to meet this requirement, as are those who frequently move between formal- and informal-sector work. Low-income workers who have spent their careers in the informal sector may be left out entirely (see Arenas de Mesa and Bertranou 1997). In short, we have gained efficiency and cut fiscal deficits, but the single largest component of social spending has an extremely weak redistributive impact.

Health. Health reform is following a similar pattern of improved efficiency through greater privatization and cost recovery. Here, the problem is compounded by dualism: in Argentina, 86 percent of care received by the upper two quintiles occurs in private clinics and hospitals while 62 percent of visits by the bottom quintile are to public clinics.

In the early 1990s, Argentina decentralized and transferred federal and provincial health care to the municipalities. To address the problem of deficits, some provinces created the concept of the fiscally autonomous hospital. The new autonomy includes the right to bill insurers directly and to retain a part of the earnings. (Most formal-sector workers are insured through occupationally based health plans known as *Obras sociales*.) Control over billing is, of course, essential to well-managed hospitals that can recover a larger share of expenditures from those who are insured or able to pay (see World Bank 1997).

The real challenge, however, lies in financing the care of the bottom quintile. Several provinces have avoided instituting hospital autonomy for fear of discrimination against the uninsured part of the population. The trend toward privatization and fiscal autonomy raises efficiency in the provision of services. To assure equity, a complementary program for the poor—such as a voucher scheme—needs further development and funding.

We also need to keep in mind that for the poorest Latin Americans, health policy can take many forms, including the provision of sanitation or the extension of public awareness campaigns to reduce infant mortality. Such policies have been credited with a 50 percent decrease in São Paulo's infant mortality rate between 1980 and 1993 (Torres 1997). At the margin, the most efficient use of resources may lie in more preventive care, particularly in very poor communities. Yet regionally, access to safe water increased only from 75 percent to 77 percent between 1982 and 1995 (World Bank 1999c).

Education. In education, we see reforms that go beyond merely closing deficits and improving efficiency. Most countries in the region have increased their spending on education (as a percentage of GDP) as a means of raising the productivity of the poor.

Mexico stands out for its recent commitment to primary education: expenditures per primary student have risen from 4.4 percent of per capita GDP to 11.9 percent. The government's new poverty program, Progresa, ties cash assistance to educational attendance; it also oversees an extensive school breakfast program that feeds 4.4 million children.[6] As Progresa and comparable programs have taken hold, the primary school dropout rate has fallen from 5.3 percent of enrolled students in 1990 to just 2.9 percent, and the net enrollment ratio of secondary school students has risen to 51 percent. Strikingly, primary school enrollment among indigenous Mexican children rose 30 percent between 1990 and 1995, and the gap in primary school enrollment between extremely poor and nonpoor children is now negligible (see Table 3). The crucial inequities now lie at the secondary school level.

As impressive as this progress is, there is still much to be done to achieve equity in access to education, in Mexico and elsewhere. Progresa's budget is less than a billion dollars. For every peso that the Mexican government spends on a student in the top two deciles, it spends fifty centavos on a student in the lowest decile. Universities still absorb a substantial amount of resources in education. In Argentina, public expenditures in 1996 per university student were $1887, compared with $808 per primary student. In Brazil, the 2 percent of students attending universities consume 60 percent of the federal education budget and 23 percent of all public educational expenditures. This heavy subsidization of tertiary education is widely regarded as regressive, for its beneficiaries include graduates of private secondary schools who can anticipate high future earnings. A system of tuition fees combined with scholarships for the lower-income quintiles would be much more equitable, but political opposition has hindered the transition to such a scheme.

TABLE 3: **Mexico: School Enrollment by Poverty Status, 1996**

	Percent
Primary (6–11 years old)	
Extreme	93.3
Moderate	96.0
Nonpoor	96.1
Secondary (12–14 years old)	
Extreme	37.9
Moderate	64.8
Nonpoor	79.1
Upper Secondary (15–17 years old)	
Extreme	14.5
Moderate	36.0
Nonpoor	58.0
University (18–24 years old)	
Extreme	1.8
Moderate	6.4
Nonpoor	22.0

Source: World Bank (1999a, 28), based on data from the Mexican National Institute of Statistics, Geography, and Information (ENIGH)

The decentralization of education also threatens to undermine equity, even as it improves the efficiency of educational programs in middle-class communities by encouraging local participation. In Mexico, federal allocations to states continue to be based on historical practice rather than need, and thus the six states that account for 46 percent of the illiterate receive only 33 percent of federally funded state grants aimed at primary education.

Brazil's constitution requires the federal government to spend 18 percent of its revenues on education, with at least 30 percent of this spending on primary education. In addition, a quarter of all state and municipal revenues must be applied to education. Municipalities and states manage the primary school system, largely with their own resources and shares of federal tax revenue. Although Congress created two funds to address inequalities in primary education, the National Education Development and Maintenance Fund (FUNDEF) and Dinheiro na Escola (Money to Schools), the size of these transfers is tiny and they have done little to alleviate regional disparities in expenditure level. As a result, the richest municipalities spend up to twenty-eight times that spent in the poorest communities on primary education (World Bank 1999b).[7]

The overdue improvements in education are bringing the region closer to educational outcomes typical of other middle-income regions. More is being done to promote primary education, but substantial inequities remain. Despite a well-established link between education and growth, the funding of education is overshadowed by the burden of social security. The numbers from Brazil are telling: between 1990 and 1995, spending on education rose by 9 percent while spending on social security rose by 90 percent.

Conclusions

There have been impressive strides in Latin America's fight against poverty, particularly in efforts to raise primary school enrollment. But the overall picture suggests little evidence of a consensus to make poverty alleviation the central objective of social policy. The middle class demanded and got greater efficiency in the programs that it benefits from; the poor have not been equally effective in their political mobilization. The funding of targeted programs remains far too small, and the trend toward greater efficiency through privatization and decentralization has added few redistributive functions compared with the old social programs.

Latin America has long been recognized as the world's most inequitable region: on average the richest 10 percent of Latin Americans receive 45 percent of income, and the poorest 20 percent receive 4 percent. Inequality increased during the 1980s, and growth in the 1990s has not been sufficient to correct that trend. Indeed, many of the poor believe that the past ten years have made them worse off.

In 1999, Latin America has seen its worst recession in ten years, casting doubt on both the benefits of economic reform and the prospects for growth as an antidote to poverty. In such an unequal region, high unemployment brings risks of political instability. So far, at least, the evidence is that the middle class refuses to give up its social welfare benefits. Yet if nothing is done to make voting booths more meaningful to the poor, economic progress and the development of civil society will falter. Where will the money come from for substantial programs to attack poverty? That is a challenge for the participants in this conference to address.

Notes

1   This paper is based on work done with Eliana Cardoso. I am grateful to the World Bank for support of this research, as well as to Mirjam Schoening, Claudia Sulpeveda, and Hongyu Liu for assistance. I am solely responsible for the views and opinions expressed.

2 Public social expenditures include the consolidated government spending on the social sectors (education, health, nutrition, social welfare, housing, and water and sanitation) and social insurance (social security, health funds, and unemployment insurance).

3 Regionally, the growth of social spending fell from 6.4 percent in the first half of the 1990s to only 3.3 percent in 1996 and 1997.

4 These estimates do not reflect the fact that payroll taxes are shifted forward to prices, implying that poor consumers also share in the burden of finance. Furthermore, high payroll taxes reduce formal sector employment and reallocate workers to the informal sector, reducing wages (see Clements 1997).

5 See Kay (1997, 48–51) for a discussion of Chile's pension reform. No other country has gone as far as Chile in privatizing pension plans.

6 A second, much smaller program, Estímulos a la Educación Básica, also ties cash stipends to school attendance.

7 FUNDEF puts a floor on per-student spending in primary school, with federal government stepping in to maintain this floor if necessary. The Dinheiro na Escola program provides money directly to primary schools for nonsalary expenditures on a per capita basis, with higher amounts going to schools in poorer regions.

References

Arenas de Mesa, Alberto, and Fabio Bertranou. 1997. "Learning from Social Security Reforms: Two Different Cases, Chile and Argentina." *World Development* 25, no. 3: 329–48.

Clements, Benedict. 1997. "Income Distribution and Social Expenditure in Brazil." International Monetary Fund Working Paper WP/97/120.

Cominetti, Rosella, and Gonzalo Ruiz. 1998. *Evolución del Gasto Público Social en América Latina: 1980–1995.* Cuadernos de la CEPAL 80, United Nations Economic Commission for Latin America, Santiago.

International Monetary Fund. 1998. *International Financial Statistics 1998 Yearbook.* Washington, D.C.

Kay, Stephen J. 1997. "The Chile Con." *The American Prospect* (July–August 1997): 48–51.

Torres, Haroldo G. 1997. "Social Policies in the 'Lost Decade': Evidence from the Case of São Paulo, Brazil." Harvard University, Center for Population Studies, December.

United Nations Economic Commission for Latin America and the Caribbean. 1999. *CEPAL News* 19:6.

World Bank. 1997. *Argentina: Facing the Challenge of Health Insurance Reform,* Report 16402-AR, Washington, D.C.

———. 1999a. "Earnings Inequality after Mexico's Economic and Educational Reforms." Mimeo. Washington, D.C.

———. 1999b. "Social Expenditure in Selected States: Brazil." Mimeo. Washington, D.C.

———. 1999c. *World Development Indicators 1999.* CD-ROM. Washington, D.C.

Administrative Reform in Brazil

CLÁUDIA COSTIN
Brazilian Secretariate of State for
Administration and Government Property

One of the greatest challenges facing governments in the 1990s has been to reform their political and administrative institutions in response to the demands of the new world order. Economic globalization, resulting from (among other things) the fall of the Berlin Wall as well as from advances in communication and computer technology, has imposed open markets. Meeting this challenge requires the establishment of creative organizations with flexible decision-making systems that can keep pace with the speed and flow of information. In the face of this process, the state-led development model has collapsed.

At the end of the 1980s and the beginning of the 1990s, neoliberal rhetoric was prominent in the debate over alternative roles of the state. The banner of the "minimum state" was raised as a solution to the crisis. However, international experience has demonstrated the fragility of such conservative guidelines in increasingly complex societies. In fact, not one of the developed countries that we studied while planning administrative reform in Brazil had experienced a decline in public expenditures (measured as a percentage of GDP) in recent years. This was especially the case in countries with weak economic performance, high unemployment, poverty, and weak state capacity for implementing public policies.

After successfully fighting hyperinflation, the Cardoso administration decided in early 1995 that the way out of the crisis would be to reconstruct the state to reflect a new management model. Steep cost reduction and control, decentralization, partnership, autonomy, accountability, efficiency, quality, administrative transparency, and accountability were to become fundamental values. These goals were codified in the Master Plan of the Reform of the State Apparatus, drafted by the Ministry of Administration and Reform of the State.

From Crisis to Reconstruction of the State in Brazil

In the previous economic model in Brazil, the state had two basic functions: to decrease the cost of capital production through investment in infrastructure for the private sector, such as steel production, energy, transportation, and road construction (activities that were implemented by public enterprises) and to generate employment and income, especially through patronage or patrimonialism. Production of goods and services to be traded in the market was also important since the private sector arrived late in the country and did not have the capital for big investments. This activity was also performed by state-owned companies. Delivering public services to the citizenry was not viewed as a state responsibility.

Thus, except for public enterprises, the state in Brazil was not designed to perform well. Efficiency was not even mentioned in the article of the Constitution that listed the values that should infuse public administration. The main point of that article was to create employment and treat civil servants in a fair and uniform manner.

It is important to keep this fact in mind when we think about the reconstruction of the state in Brazil. The reform team is not only dealing with fiscal measures such as cutting public expenditures. State reform involves something much more complex—changing the paradigm from a state that intervenes in production and is a depository of personnel to that of a state that delivers public services, formulates public policies, and regulates the private operation of utilities.

In Brazil, the emergence of the state as a producer of goods and services goes back to the 1930s, with the implementation of the federal government modernization project, which aimed to consolidate national industry. To this end, the state increased its intervention and consequently its economic and social functions, resulting in continuous growth of the state apparatus. It should be noted that this increase led to growth in personnel costs and the need to raise revenues and expenditures.

The crisis of the Brazilian state in the 1990s reflected the exhaustion of the interventionist state model. This model, often referred to as import-substitution industrialization, was fundamental to the development of the industrial sector. In addition to the failure of import-substitution industrialization, there is a growing perception that the corporatist model that has infused the Brazilian bureaucracy since the 1930s is no longer working. Rising expectations about the performance of the state have put pressure on Brazil's public administration to assume a more citizen-oriented approach.

The crisis of the Brazilian state has four basic components. First, there is the fiscal crisis, which reflects the insufficiency of public savings to match the investments that society demands. This aspect of the crisis is more evident now, not only for the federal government but also at the state and municipal levels, because the government can no longer rely upon inflation as a tool of adjustment. It is no longer possible to postpone paying suppliers or to freeze civil servants' salaries in order to let inflation adjust unbalanced budgets. In addition, the growing financial burden of the social security system became unbearable. The gap between what civil servants contribute and what they receive for relatively generous benefits—including early retirement pensions for workers and their survivors—amounts to approximately US$18 billion per year.

If one looks back thirty years, it becomes clear that the fiscal crisis originated with the indebtedness of state-owned firms, debt that was incurred in the 1970s because of high levels of investment with low rates of return; the international liquidity crisis; the hike in petroleum prices; a decline in interest rates (which encouraged indebtedness) and then their later rise and the debt crisis of the early 1980s; the inflationary corrosion of public revenues; the enormous expansion of domestic debt; and the disproportionate increase in financial and personnel expenditures.

The fiscal crisis has imposed the need for restricting public expenditures during the 1990s. Furthermore, there has been increasing awareness within the government and throughout society that increasing social expenditures didn't necessarily generate more or better service. The solution for improving the poor quality of government services that the Brazilian public receives is not spending more but spending more effectively. In short, the key is to improve the quality of public expenditures.

It is important to note that in some respects, the crisis had a positive impact on Brazil. For example, the federal, state, and municipal governments are managing their payrolls with newfound austerity. As previously mentioned, they can no longer freeze salaries and delay payments to suppliers in order to balance their books. The crisis proved to be an opportunity to make necessary changes in the public sector. The tasks of modernizing public administration and correcting distortions in the profile and composition of the workforce are now starting to be undertaken. Yet there is still a poor distribution of human resources, with excess personnel in operational and administrative support activities, and a shortage of well-trained technicians specializing in formulating, implementing, and evaluating public policy, which is the central role of the federal government.

The second dimension of the crisis of the Brazilian state arose with the erosion of the model of state intervention in the economy. Regardless of the governing ideology, the model of the state as both producer of goods and services and provider of low-cost production capital is being challenged. The boundaries of privatization in Brazil are still being defined. It is up to the public power to discern what can be privatized, and up to society to exert accountability over this process. The state no longer plays the role of the producer of goods and services (now offered by the market); instead it exercises the functions of regulation of natural monopolies and defender of competition. This does not mean, however, that the thesis of the minimum state is correct. On the contrary, the state has to be strong in forming public policies that meet the needs of the country's population. As I mentioned previously, in no country has public expenditure as a proportion of GDP fallen. The thesis of the minimum state is not only incorrect but inapplicable.

On the contrary, the state has to establish strong regulatory agencies. Brazil was late in beginning this process. The process of privatizing state-owned utilities was started even before the first regulatory agencies were up and running. We now have to rush to catch up in consolidating these institutions, in a context where most utilities have already been privatized, and there is intense social pressure to have public agencies ensure the quality of the services being delivered.

The third dimension of the crisis of the Brazilian state is related to the challenge of consolidating democracy. During the military regime, there was a significant increase in social demands, which had been unmet for more than two decades. With the process of redemocratization, there was increasing awareness of these social needs. However, the explosion of social demands could not be met due to the fiscal crisis of the state. The result was a combination of both revolt and frustration, as learning democracy has proven to be a difficult process. In a totalitarian regime, it is easy to reform the state: the legislature is closed, the press is censored, individual rights are suppressed, laws are made null and void, and arbitrary measures are imposed. However, in a democratic regime, meeting social demands requires reforms that must be negotiated democratically with various actors. Resistance and lack of understanding are natural, since reforms affect the interests of specific groups. The patronage culture, which still has strong roots in the state and society, is resistant to reforms. The bureaucratic culture also resists change because bureaucrats are aware that reform will diminish their power. In this context, reformers must on the one hand be firm and consistent in promoting needed reforms, but on the other hand they must learn to negotiate and respect the mandate of elected representatives.

The fourth dimension of the crisis of the Brazilian state encompasses the management of the state apparatus. The deteriorating performance of the state apparatus in the past two decades is due mainly to three factors: first, the fiscal crisis, which imposed strong budgetary restrictions and reduced investment capacity; second, the great expansion of social demands as a result of the political process of redemocratization and the emergence of new social and urban groups; and third, the exhaustion of the bureaucratic model of management, which lagged behind the managerial standards of the private sector and failed to respond to social demands.

The country still suffers from a tendency to try to solve cultural and managerial problems by means of issuing new rules and regulations. As I said before, the state was not designed to perform efficiently in Brazil, so the fact that these rules limit the efficiency of public agencies did not apparently worry legislators. Their primary means of fighting corruption was through issuing more and more laws. However, the government has not been effective in stopping wrongdoing. It has also limited state managers' freedom of action. In addition, because of a complex institutional framework, state procurement procedures are flawed; the government fails to recruit skilled civil servants, offers little training, and has archaic work routines.

Since 1995, the Cardoso administration has been promoting a series of reforms with a view toward overcoming the crisis of the state. We can divide the drive toward state reform into two periods. During President Cardoso's first term in office, the focus was on constitutional reform. Constitutional Amendment 19 of the Administrative Reform Act removed legal obstacles to significant organizational change. The 1998 congressional approval of the Administrative Reform Act amendment has laid the groundwork for a long-term cap on personnel expenditures and for streamlining civil service at all levels of government. Most of the legislation regulating the implementation of the reform has been passed recently by Congress, and approval of the remaining enabling laws is expected soon. These measures include a law that places a ceiling on payroll expenditures as a share of net revenues at all levels of government and a law mandating the dismissal of civil servants if these limits are exceeded. A number of states and municipalities have reduced spending on personnel to comply with the new law. The federal government, for its part, has taken steps to reduce its payroll through administrative improvements, including steps to identify and correct payroll irregularities. It is currently reviewing federal salary scales in order to achieve greater parity with the private sector as well as taking additional steps to streamline the civil service and introduce additional flexibility in the management of human resources. The goal is to treat civil servants as well-trained, well-paid, motivated professionals. Although these measures are unlikely to yield substantial savings in the short run, they will significantly contribute to improving the quality and efficiency of public administration over time. There are now more training programs for public officials, incentive programs for public school employees, and programs to promote greater managerial autonomy, based on the principles of transparency and accountability. One major element of this initiative was the launching of the professional training policy. Out of a total of 508,000 federal civil servants, 390,000 were trained during the last four years. Together with professionalization, a process of fostering a new culture of public service directed toward better performance has begun.

Currently, the public sector is experiencing a change of attitude, and the great improvement in performance is due to the extension of the entrepreneurial management model. There is now a consensus that it is necessary to promote entrepreneurial management of resources in order to ensure sustainable growth. Budgeting is no longer an act of fiction but is instead oriented toward achieving targets and results. A new emphasis on the training and performance of managers has been incorporated into this process, along with greater transparency and public accountability.

About the Authors

Fábio de Oliveira Barbosa is the secretary of the National Treasury in Brazil. Prior to assuming his current position in July 1999, he was the deputy secretary of the National Treasury from July 1995 to June 1999. Secretary Barbosa has had an extensive career in public service: he has served as special adviser to the minister of finance (March–July 1995); adviser to the executive director in the World Bank Group's counsel of administration (November 1992–February 1995); general coordinator of fiscal policy in the Ministry of Finance's Special Secretariat of Political Economy (March 1990–May 1991), among other positions. He holds a master's degree in economic theory from the University of Brasília.

Carlos Boloña is president of the San Ignacio de Loyola University in Lima, Peru, and chairman of the Free Market Economy Institute in Lima. From 1991 to 1993, he served as Peru's minister of economy and finance. Dr. Boloña chairs and serves on the boards of several private corporations in Peru and has been a consultant for the World Bank, USAID, and other organizations. He is the author of *Cambio de Rumbo: un Programa Económico para los 90*, a work detailing Peru's economic reforms in the early 1990s. Dr. Boloña holds a Ph.D. in economics from Oxford University.

Michael J. Chriszt is director of Latin America analysis at the Federal Reserve Bank of Atlanta. His primary responsibilities include monitoring and reporting on economic, financial, and political developments in foreign economies. His research interests include fiscal policy in Latin America and international lending arrangements. His work has appeared in various Federal Reserve Bank of Atlanta publications, including the *Economic Review*. He holds a master's degree in political science from Miami University in Ohio and has completed the management training program at Duke University.

Cláudia Costin served until recently as Brazil's secretary of state for administration and government property and is now a private consultant on public sector reform issues. In the past she has served as Brazil's minister of federal administration and state reform as well as director of planning and analysis for the economy ministry in Brazil. Dr. Costin also has extensive teaching experience at the University of Brasília and other institutions. She holds a doctorate from the School of Business Administration at the Getúlio Vargas Foundation in São Paulo.

Juan Carlos Echeverry-Garzon is director of the macroeconomic analysis unit in Colombia's National Planning Department. Dr. Echeverry has extensive experience in Colombia's central bank and has been a consultant with the Inter-American Development Bank. He has written widely on macroeconomic issues in Colombia, with a special emphasis on savings and inflation. Dr. Echeverry holds a Ph.D. in economics from New York University.

Robert A. Eisenbeis is senior vice president and director of research at the Federal Reserve Bank of Atlanta, serving as chief adviser to the Bank president on monetary policy. Prior to joining the Bank, Dr. Eisenbeis was the Wachovia Professor of Banking at the Kenan-Flagler Business School at the University of North Carolina at Chapel Hill. His prior experience includes work with the Board of Governors of the Federal Reserve System and the Federal Deposit Insurance Corporation. His work has appeared in the *Journal of Finance*, the *Journal of Money, Credit, and Banking*, and the *Journal of Regulatory Economics*, among other publications. Dr. Eisenbeis holds a Ph.D. in economics from the University of Wisconsin at Madison.

Andrés Fontana is undersecretary of state for strategic policies with the Presidency of Argentina. His research interests include defense and international security issues. Dr. Fontana has held teaching positions at the University of Buenos Aires, the Catholic University of Córdoba, the Argentine Foreign Service Institute, and the University of North Carolina. He has been a fellow of the Social Science Research Council and of the Kellogg Institute at the University of Notre Dame. Dr. Fontana holds a Ph.D. in government from the University of Texas at Austin.

Francisco Gil-Díaz is chief executive officer of the telecommunications firm Avantel, a joint venture between the Mexican financial group Banamex Accival and MCI WorldCom. Dr. Gil-Díaz has been chief economist and deputy governor of the Bank of Mexico, as well as undersecretary of the Treasury in charge of tax policy and administration. The former chair of the economics department at Instituto Tecnológico Autónomo de México (ITAM), he has published extensively on public finance, exchange rate policy, and macroeconomic management. Dr. Gil-Díaz holds a Ph.D. in economics from the University of Chicago.

Lawrence S. Graham is director of the Brazil Center and professor of government at the University of Texas at Austin. His interests lie in public policy and comparative politics, and his current research centers on customs administration along the U.S.-Mexican border as well as regional development policy in Europe and Latin America. Dr. Graham's recent books include *Politics and Government: A Brief Introduction* and *The Portuguese Military and the State: Rethinking Transitions in Europe and Latin America*. Dr. Graham holds a Ph.D. from the University of Florida.

Jack Guynn is president and chief executive officer of the Federal Reserve Bank of Atlanta. During his thirty-five year career with the Atlanta Fed, Mr. Guynn has held responsibilities for payments operations, bank supervision, lending, and human resources. As president, Mr. Guynn is responsible for all the Bank's activities, including monetary policy, supervision and regulation, and operations. He also serves on the Federal Reserve System's chief monetary policy body, the Federal Open Market Committee. Mr. Guynn earned a bachelor's degree in industrial engineering and has completed management training programs at Harvard University and the Georgia Institute of Technology.

Ann Helwege is associate professor in the Department of Urban and Environmental Policy at Tufts University. She also teaches at the Fletcher School of Law and Diplomacy at Tufts University. Dr. Helwege has written several books on major economic issues facing Latin America and on economic adjustment in Cuba in the aftermath of the Cold War. Her current research areas include poverty, economic stabilization, and environmental policy in Latin America. Dr. Helwege holds a B.A. in political science and a Ph.D. in economics from the State University of New York at Buffalo.

Stephen Kay is an economic analyst with the Latin America Research Group at the Federal Reserve Bank of Atlanta. Dr. Kay's research interests include the politics of pension reform in Latin America. His work has appeared in *Comparative Politics*, the *Journal of European Social Policy*, and the *Journal of Interamerican Studies and World Affairs*. He has testified twice before committees in the U.S. House of Representatives as an expert witness. Prior to joining the Atlanta Fed research department, Dr. Kay taught at the California State University at Fullerton and the University of California at Los Angeles. Dr. Kay holds a Ph.D. in political science from the University of California at Los Angeles.

Elizabeth McQuerry is senior economic analyst with the Latin America Research Group at the Federal Reserve Bank of Atlanta. Dr. McQuerry's research interests include public sector reform and banking issues in Latin America, with a particular focus on Brazil. Her writing has appeared in the *American Political Science Review*, and her article "Banking Sector Rescue in Mexico" is in the third quarter 1999 issue of the Atlanta Fed's *Economic Review*. Dr. McQuerry holds a Ph.D. in government from the University of Texas at Austin.

Verónica Navas-Ospina is a junior research economist in the macroeconomic analysis unit of Colombia's National Planning Department. She received both B.A. and M.A. degrees in economics from the Andes University in Bogotá, Colombia. Her research interests include international economics, institutional economics and public sector reform.

Arturo C. Porzecanski is the New York–based managing director and Americas chief economist at ING Barings, the investment-banking arm of the ING Group, and the managing editor of the company's flagship publication, the *Emerging Markets Weekly Report*. Prior to joining ING, he was the chief emerging markets economist at Kidder, Peabody & Co. and the chief economist at Republic National Bank of New York. He has also served as a long-time senior economist at J.P. Morgan & Co. Inc., a research economist at the Center for Latin American Monetary Studies in Mexico City, and a visiting economist at the International Monetary Fund. Dr. Porzecanski holds a Ph.D. in economics from the University of Pittsburgh.

Ben Ross Schneider is associate professor in the political science department at Northwestern University, in Evanston, Illinois, where he teaches courses in comparative politics, political economy, and Latin American politics. His current research interests include business politics in Latin America and administrative reform in developing countries. He is the author of *Politics within the State: Elite Bureaucrats and Industrial Policy in Authoritarian Brazil*. Dr. Schneider holds a Ph.D. in political science from the University of California at Berkeley.

Graham Stock is vice president for international fixed-income research with Chase Securities Inc. in New York, where he has primary responsibility for economic and political analysis of Latin America. Previously, he was a senior economist for the Latin America team of the Economist Intelligence Unit (EIU) as well as the EIU's deputy director of forecasting. As a fellow of the Overseas Development Institute, Mr. Stock provided fiscal policy advisory services to the government of Papua, New Guinea. Mr. Stock earned an M.A. degree in development economics from the University of Manchester, England.

Kurt Weyland is assistant professor of political science at Vanderbilt University and is currently a visiting scholar fellow at the Woodrow Wilson Center in Washington, D.C. His research interests include social policy, democracy, and economic reform in Latin America. Dr. Weyland is the author of *Democracy Without Equity: Failures of Reform in Brazil*. His work has appeared in *Comparative Politics*, the *Latin American Research Review*, and other publications. Dr. Weyland holds a Ph.D. in political science from Stanford University.